MANNERS FOR MEN

MANNERS
FOR MEN

BY MRS. HUMPHRY
("MADGE" OF "TRUTH")

London
JAMES BOWDEN
10, HENRIETTA STREET,
COVENT GARDEN, W.C.
1897

MEMBER OF
INDEPENDENT PUBLISHERS GUILD

© 1993 PRYOR PUBLICATIONS
75 Dargate Road, Yorkletts, Whitstable,
Kent CT5 3AE, England.

Tel. & Fax: (0227) 274655

Specialist in Facsimile Reproductions.

A CIP Record for this book is available from the British Library

ISBN 0 946014 23 X

*Pryor Publications wish to thank
Peter Stockham for his advice and assistance
in the publication of this book.*

MANNERS FOR MEN

FIRST EDITION	.	.	.	.	*February, 1897.*
SECOND EDITION	.	.	.	.	*March, 1897.*
REPRINTED	.	.	.	.	*May, 1994.*
REPRINTED	.	.	.	.	*November, 1994.*
REPRINTED	.	.	.	.	*January, 1995.*

Printed and bound by
Whitstable Litho Printers Ltd., Whitstable.

CONTENTS.

CONTENTS.

MANNERS FOR MEN.

WOMAN'S IDEAL MAN.

I suppose there was never yet a woman who had not somewhere set up on a pedestal in her brain an ideal of manhood. He is by no means immutable, this paragon. On the contrary, he changes very often.

The ideal changes with the idealist. If, however, the woman whose ideal he is grows upward in every way as she grows older, then these changes all go to improve him, and by the time he is finished he is a very fine creature. He never is finished till the brain of his creator ceases to work, till she has added her last touch to him, and has laid down the burden of life and gone elsewhere, perhaps to some happy land where ideals are more frequently realised than ever happens here.

Like every other woman, I have my ideal of manhood. The difficulty is to describe it. First of all, he *My ideal man.* must be a gentleman; but that means so much that it, in its turn, requires explanation.

Gentleness and moral strength combined must be the salient characteristics of the "gentleman," together with that polish that is never acquired but in one way : constant association with those so happily placed that they have enjoyed the influences of education and refinement all through their lives. He must be thoughtful for others, kind to women and children and all helpless things, tenderhearted to the old and the poor and the unhappy, but never foolishly weak in giving where gifts do harm instead of good—his brain must be as fine as his heart, in fact. There are few such men ; but they do exist. I know one or two. Reliable as rocks, judicious in every action, dependable in trifles as well as the large affairs of life, full of mercy and kindness to others, affectionate and well-loved in their homes, their lives are pure and kindly.

A man's brain should be as fine as his heart.

It was once said by a clever man that no one could be a gentleman all round who had not knocked about the world and associated with all sorts and conditions of men, high and low, rich and poor, good and bad. Experiences like these are like the processes for refining gold. The man who emerges unharmed from the fire of poverty and its associations, and who retains his independent manliness

The furnace of experience.

in relations with those high-placed, must have within him a fibre of strength that is the true essence of manliness. So many, alas! go down, down, when "puirtith cauld" touches them with her terrible, chilly finger. And so many become obsequious and subservient, false to themselves, in dealings with those above them.

Well! my ideal does neither. He is always true to himself, and "cannot then be false to any man." And he must have a sense of humour, too, otherwise he would be far from perfect. How life is brightened by a sense of fun! Think of what breakfast, lunch, and dinner would be if all were to be as solemn and as serious as some folk would have it!

Humour an essential.

If good manners are not practised at home, but are allowed to lie by until occasion calls upon their wearer to assume them, they are sure to be a bad fit when donned. It may be a trifle of the smallest to acquire a habit of saying "if you please" and "thank you" readily, but it is no trifling defect in a young man to fail to do so. If he does not jump up to open the door for his mother or sister, he may omit to do so some day when the neglect will tell against him in the estimation of those to please whom he would gladly give much. Carelessness in dress and personal appearance

On behaviour in one's own home.

3

amount to bad manners. In the home there is sometimes a disagreeable negligence in this respect. At the breakfast-table unkempt hair, untended finger-nails, and a far from immaculate collar are occasionally to be seen, especially on late-comers who do not practise the ingratiating politeness of punctuality. Lounging, untidy habits are another form of bad manners. The ill-bred young man smokes all over the house, upstairs and downstairs, and even in his mother's drawing-room.

The ill-bred young man at home.

He may be traced from room to room by the litter of newspapers and magazines he leaves behind him. The present fashion of taking one's reading in pills, so to speak, snatching it in scrappy paragraphs from weekly miscellanies, is but too favourable to this lack of order. In this young man's own room there is chaos. The maids have endless trouble in clearing up after him. His tobacco is spilled over tables, chairs, and carpets. His handkerchiefs, ties, socks, and collars are lying about in every corner of the room. He is too indolent even to put his boots outside the door at night that they may be cleaned in the morning. To save himself trouble he bangs all the doors instead of gently latching them. And yet, perhaps, if he could but realise that all this is " bad manners," he would become as neat as he is now the reverse, and would be as decorative

4

at table as he is, at the present moment, unornamental.

It is not only young men whose standard of behaviour in the home is a low one. Masters of the house, fathers of families, men of middle age, who are terribly put out if any one fails in duty to them, are sometimes conspicuously ill-bred in everyday matters. They are late for every meal, to the discomfort of the other members of the family and the great inconvenience of the servants. Polite to the world outside, they are brusque and disagreeable in their manner at home : rough to the servants, rude to their wives, and irritable with their children. Sometimes a good heart and considerable family affection are hidden away behind all this, but the families of such men would be very glad to compound for a little less affection and hidden goodness and rather more gentleness and outward polish.

"Young" men not alone culpable.

Apart from faults of temper, men fall into careless habits of speech and manner at home, and one form of this, viz., habitually using strong language in the presence of women and children, is particularly offensive. Besides, it defeats itself ; for if the forcible expressions are intended to express disapprobation, they soon become weak and powerless to do so, because they are used on every possible occa-

On strong language.

sion. After a time they lose all meaning.

I know a family where there are sons and daughters, the latter charming and in every respect young gentlewomen. But the sons fall far below their level. They come to the door with thundering knocks that make every one in the house start disagreeably with surprise, walk through the hall without introducing their muddy boots to either scraper or doormat, sit down to meals without the usual preliminary of handwashing and hair-brushing, and are altogether rough and unpresentable. If friends call at the house these young men rush away from the chance of encountering them ; or, if they cannot help meeting them, they blush scarlet, look very *gauche* and uncomfortable, and feel miserable. They knock things over out of pure awkwardness, and never realise that the secret of the whole matter is the want of self-training. Girls are animated by a greater wish to please, an amiable desire that need not be confounded with vanity, and this wish has led the sisters of these young men to practise those small acts of daily self-denial which after awhile produce the highest self-culture so far as manners go. What is habitual neatness but constant coercion of human nature's innate indolence ? What is polite-

A typical family.

The secret of the whole matter.

The feminine motive.

ness in the home but the outcome of affection and self-respect, and the suppression of all those natural instincts of self-seeking that, allowed their way, produce the worst manners in the world ?

If any young man desires to be a perfect gentleman, he must begin in his own home. It is delightful to see some young men unobtrusively attentive to their sisters, watchful of every need of their father and mother, cheerful and pleasant in their manner, full of fun and brightness, yet never losing the gentleness that denotes the fine nature, and so beloved in the home for all these endearing qualities, that when they leave it they are sadly missed. The father misses them for the pleasant companionship ; the sisters miss them for the boyish spirits and the exuberant fun that never exceeds the bounds of good taste and refinement ; and the mother misses them more than any one else, for no one better than she knows how many times a day her boys have set aside their own wishes in deference to hers, quietly, silently, unostentatiously —in a word, out of pure good manners, in the deepest, highest, truest sense of the words. Such gentle, virile natures look out at the world through the countenance, which is a letter of recommendation to them wherever they go.

The young man every one loves.

"Gentle, yet virile."

I have but faintly sketched my ideal.

7

The following pages may fill in the remaining touches.

Many men who go out into the world while still very young to earn their living have few oppor- tunities of acquiring a know- ledge of social observances.

Difficulties in the way.

Leaving home when boys, at an age when they are utterly careless of such things as etiquette and the "nice con- duct of a cane," they live in lodgings or at boarding-houses of the cheaper sort, where the amenities of exist- ence have to yield to its practicalities. Meals are served in a fashion that means despatch rather than elegance, economy rather than taste, and very few hints can be picked up for the guidance of young fellows when they enter the homes of friends and ac- quaintances. Their anxiety to fall in accurately and easily with the observances of those they meet on such occa- sions is as great as it is natural. They know well that to fail in these trifling acts of omission and commission is tacitly to acknowledge that they are unversed in the ways of good society. There is not necessarily any snobbishness in this. A man may be per- fectly manly and yet most unwilling to show himself inferior in any way to others of the class to which he belongs by birth and education. Even should

"Where amenities yield to prac- ticalities."

The penalty of ignorance.

The aspirant is not neces- sarily a snob.

those with whom he occasionally associates be his superiors, is he not right to try to rise? Culture may mean little or nothing to the un-cultured. Polish may be an empty word to the un-polished. But they are realities, and go far to produce an inward and corresponding refinement of mind and spirit.

Culture and polish are realities.

There are thousands of young men in London alone at this very moment who are longing to acquire the ease and *aplomb* of good society. The desire is worthy of all encouragement. Only those with real good in them can feel it. The men who are destitute of it are those who associate with their inferiors, contentedly accept a low moral standard, adopt a mode of speech and action that is coarse and rough, and finally let themselves down to the frequenting of public-houses and places of amusement, where the entertainment has been carefully planned to suit the uneducated, the low-born, and others whose vitiated taste leads them to dislike what is lovely and of good report, and to revel in the reverse.

The desire to rise deserves encouragement.

But, unfortunately, many a good fellow has been driven to seek companionship with those beneath him by the very difficulty he experiences in getting on in society. He fancies that his small solecisms are the subject of

Men to be pitied.

9

observation and comment, and he suffers agonies of *mauvaise honte.* Girls often laugh very unkindly at shy youths, when they might find opportunities of acting the good angel to them, and by the exercise of tact screening from observation those failures in good manners which are inevitable to the inexperienced. When he finds himself the butt of a few giggling girls, a young man feels miserably uncomfortable and humiliated, and he vows to himself that he will never again put himself in the way of such annoyance. Consequently he cuts good society, not realising that he would very soon overcome these initial difficulties and feel at home in it.

A word to girls.

He must find amusement somewhere. It is only natural to youth to crave it. At first his taste is jarred by those inferior to him, and his fastidiousness offended by their manners. But, such is the fatal adaptability of human nature to what is bad for it, he soon becomes accustomed to all that he at first objected to, and even forgets that he had ever found anything disagreeable in it. After a few months his speech begins to assimilate the errors of those about him in his leisure hours. He uses the very expressions that jarred upon him at first. His dress and carriage deteriorate, and he is well on his way

"We first endure, then pity, then embrace."

downhill in life long before he realises that he has quitted his own level, probably for ever.

And if only he had held his own at a few gatherings, and acquired experience, even at the cost

"If he had only held his own!" of a little present pain and mortification, he would in the same interval of time be enjoying society, educating himself in its customs, and acquiring that exterior polish which comes of intimate acquaintance with its rules and ease in practising them.

Should this little manual of manners be of use to any such in enabling them to master the theory, as it

The object of this book. were, of social customs in the educated classes, it will have attained its aim. I have always felt the greatest compassion for young men when first introduced, after school and college life, to the routine of dinner, dance, and ball. I have not forgotten the days when

Those early days! shyness made my own heart sink at the prospect of a dinner-party and when the hardest task on earth was the finding of nothings to say to a partner at a ball. It is a miserable feeling of confusion and *gaucherie*, and if I can in any way avert it from others it will be a source of great gratification to me.

IN THE STREET.

THE rule of the road is a simple one, though it is often forgotten or neglected—"Keep to the right." "The rule of the road." Easy enough for women, it is complicated in the case of men by the necessity of always remaining on the kerb side of any lady they may be accompanying. Should the lady keep to the right in meeting or in passing other persons, her escort may either keep by her or go out in the road. He will be able to judge for himself which course will be advisable. His first duty is always A man's duty is always to his lady. to his companion, but that need not make him wanting in courtesy to other women. If remaining by the side of his companion should involve any inconvenience to the ladies of the other party, then he must give up his position, and go out into the roadway to let the latter pass. Should these be men, no consideration is necessary. He keeps close by his lady's side. In crowded "In crowded streets." streets he may often have to fall behind, but he should never allow any one to interpose

between her and him. Should he
pressure from the crowd become extreme, his duty is to protect her from
it as much as possible, but never by
putting his arm round her waist. A
hand on either side the lady's shoulders
is usually sufficient.

In meeting acquaintances a nod is
sufficient for a male friend, unless
his age or position is such
as to render it advisable to
raise the hat. Should a lady be with
the acquaintance, any man meeting
them must raise his hat. So must he
individual walking with the lady. The
etiquette of bowing is a simple one.
Male acquaintances always wait for
acknowledgment on the part
of female, as well as from
those men who are their
superiors in age or position.
But this does not mean that they are
shyly to look away from them and to
ignore them. On the contrary, they
must show clearly by their manner that
they are on the look-out for some sign
of recognition and are ready
to reply to it. Shyness
often interferes with this
and makes a young man
look away, and this is occasionally mis-
construed as indifference and resented
as such. The calm, quiet, collected
expression of face that suits the occasion is not achieved at once. Sometimes the over-anxiety to make a good
impression defeats itself, producing a

Salutations.

**The right of
acknowledg-
ment rests
with the lady.**

**On waiting
for acknow-
ledgment.**

blushing eagerness better suited to a girlish than a manly countenance. This, however, is a youthful fault that is not without its ingratiating side, though young men view it in themselves and in each other with unbounded scorn. This

On self-con-tempt. sentiment of self-contempt is a frequent one in young people of both sexes. Their valuation of themselves varies as much as the barometer, and is as much affected by outward causes. After a "snub," real or fancied, it goes down to zero, but as a rule it speedily recovers itself, and in most young men enjoys an agreeable thermometer of 85° or so in the shade !

The well-mannered man never puts out his hand in greeting until a lady extends hers. This is a test

Offering the hand. of good breeding that is constantly applied. To those uninitiated in the ways of society, it would naturally appear the right thing to give as cordial a greeting as possible. Therefore the hand is held out, even on introduction to a perfect stranger. This is wrong. The first move in the direction of cordiality must come from the lady, the whole code of behaviour being based on the assumption that she is the social superior. The same holds good with elders and men of higher rank. When a man is introduced to these he raises his hat and bows, though slightly. It is only to kings and princes that a low bow is made, or to those whose character and eminent position render an introduction to them a very high honour.

In introducing two men to each other the name of the inferior is mentioned first. By the inferior I mean the younger, the less important, or of lower rank. Suppose one of the two to be a familiar friend, and another a comparatively new acquaintance, then formality requires that the familiar friend shall be introduced to the other, being named first. The reason for this is that one naturally stands more on ceremony with the man one knows least. There may be counteracting circumstances, however, which would tend to reverse this order of things, but as a general rule, the social rank of both being equal, the above holds good.

Introducing men to men.

Never introduce a lady to a gentleman; but always the gentleman to the lady. That is, mention the man's name first, addressing yourself to the woman— thus: "Allow me to introduce my friend Mr. Smith, Miss Jones." And follow this up immediately by saying, "Miss Jones," addressing Mr. Smith as you do so. It is a grave solecism to begin by introducing the lady. Tyros very naturally conclude that the lady's name should be first mentioned; but on thinking it over they will soon perceive that to do so would infer that she is the lesser consideration of the two.

Introducing men to ladies.

It must always be borne in mind that the assumption of woman's social superiority lies at the root of these rules of conduct.

"Woman's social superiority."

It is bad manners to introduce people without permission. Nor must this permission be asked in the hearing of the second party. If Mr. A. wishes to know Miss B., the lady's leave must be obtained before he can be presented to her. The only exception to this rule is at a dance or ball, where introductions need not be regarded as leading to acquaintanceship. They are only for the dance, and may be ignored next day.

On permission to introduce.

Here, again, it is the lady's privilege to ignore her partner, if she choose. But if she should bow to him he must raise his hat, whether he desires to follow up the acquaintanceship or not. Objections more frequently arise on the woman's side; but should a man prefer to drop the matter he can manage to convey in his manner a disinclination to do so, and yet behave with perfect politeness. A man I knew was once introduced at a ball to a girl, with whom he had danced two or three times. Before he met her again he heard that she had been actively concerned in circulating a slander about another girl whom circumstances had misrepresented. I

On recognition after a dance.

happened to see the next meeting between the two. The girl bowed, smiled, and showed some sign of an intention to stop and talk. The man raised his hat, looked extremely solemn and unsociable, and passed on. It was enough. The girl understood that he did not wish to resume the ball-room acquaintanceship, and very probably guessed why. He did it beautifully.

Engineering an awkward point.

Before leaving the subject of the promenade, I must clearly explain that the hat must be raised even in saluting a very familiar friend, if (*a*) that friend is accompanied by a lady, and (*b*) when one is oneself accompanied by a lady, even if she be only a mother or sister. It is one of the signs of caste that a man is equally polite to his relatives as he is to the relatives of others. We all know what to think of a man who omits small social duties where his wife is concerned.

The hat and the promenade.

One's duty to one's own relatives.

Even when he proves by paying them duly to other women that he is aware of what he ought to do, he is at once set down as ill-bred—a " cad," in fact. I once saw a Lord Mayor of London enter his carriage before his wife, who scrambled in after him as though well accustomed to do so. One does not expect the refinement of good manners from

A case in point.

civic dignitaries, as a rule, but this little
action told the spectators more about
the man than they would ever have
found out in the newspapers. They at
once perceived that he was unversed
in the ways of good society.

But some one may suggest that this
may have been on some state occasion,

when his mayoral dignity
The lady first obliged him to precede his
under every
circumstance. wife. No. It was after a
wedding. And besides, can
any one fancy the Prince of Wales in
any circumstances entering his carriage
without having previously handed in
the Princess, should she be his companion ?

If accompanied by a dog, or dogs,
their owner must hold himself re-

sponsible for their good
When accom- behaviour. If his pets tres-
panied by
dogs. pass in any way he must
apologise for them, and do
his best to repair any damage they
have done. Should one of his dogs
jump on a lady and make her gown
muddy, he must offer his services and
endeavour to get rid of the traces
of the accident, if the lady wishes.
Should she show a disinclination to
accept his aid, he must at once withdraw, raising his hat as he does so.
Should his dog attack another dog he
must immediately call him off, administer correction, and apologise to the,
owner of the dog assaulted. I saw a
young man once, in these circum-

stances, beat the other dog, after his own had jumped on it and bitten its ear! He was dressed like a gentleman, but his behaviour gave a truer indication of him than did his garments.

Whistling and singing are incompatible with the conduct of a gentleman in the street, though *On whistling and singing.* this by no means applies to a quiet country road, where ceremonious bearing is not required. Nor is it permitted to wear the hands in the pockets when walking *Carriage of the hands.* in the Park, or the streets of a town or city. This is probably one of the reasons that the cane or stick is still carried, though the original cause, that of self-defence in an age that was destitute of law and order, fortunately exists no longer. There are men who would not know what to do with their hands if they had not a cane or umbrella. This is partly the fault of those who have charge of boys when they are grow- *A word to parents.* ing, and who allow them to lounge about in slovenly attitudes with their hands for ever in their pockets. Then when they begin to enter society they are quite at a loss. At schools where *And schoolmasters.* boys are regularly drilled the whole effect of the drilling is done away with by the way in which the boys are allowed to sit and stand in the most remarkable attitudes of slouching awkwardness.

It is only when they are at drill or out walking with the masters that any notice is taken of their carriage. And yet it is an important point with regard to health that the shoulders should be held well back, the chest forward, and the head up.

Should a man be so fortunate as to be of some service to any lady in the street, such as picking up a parcel or sunshade she may have dropped, or helping her out of any small difficulty, he must raise his hat and withdraw at once. Such trifling acts as these do not by any means constitute an acquaintanceship, and to remain by her side when the incident is over would look like presuming on what he had done, as though it gave him a right to her continued acknowledgments. This would be ungentlemanly.

On rendering slight services.

At the same time, these occurrences are sometimes deliberately planned by girls and women with a direct view to scraping acquaintance with young men. It is scarcely necessary to say that girls who stoop to this kind of manœuvring are hardly ever gentlewomen. Members of good families have been known to do such things in the wild exuberance of youth and high spirits, but they cannot hope to retain the respect of those who know them when they deliberately lower themselves in

On girls making advances.

such ways as these. Picking up promiscuous male acquaintances

The risk to one's good name. is a practice fraught with
danger. It cannot be denied
that girls of the lower middle
classes are often prone to it; and
there are thousands of young men who
have no feminine belongings in the
great towns and cities where they live,
and who are found responsive to this
indiscriminating mode of

The method can produce little good. making acquaintances. But
they must often hesitate
before choosing as wife a
girl who shows so little discretion as
to walk and talk with young men of
whom she knows nothing beyond what
they choose to tell her.

The seaside season is prolific in these
chance acquaintanceships—

Seaside 'Flirtations.' "flirtations," as they may
perhaps be called. Bicycling
is well known to favour them. But
as they are far removed from the
practices of the class of society to which
belong those gentlemen of whom this
little book treats, they may be dis-
missed with a few words of advice.
Should any young man become ac-
quainted with a girl in this manner,
let him show his innate chivalry by
treating her in every way as he would
wish his own sister to be

Should the man become attached. treated in similar circumstances. If he becomes at-
tached to her, let him first
find out all about her that he possibly

can, and should what he hears be encouraging, then let him ask her to introduce him to her family as a suitor for her hand. Should the girl fall in love with him, let him protect her against herself like a *preux chevalier*, like an honourable and high-minded English gentleman. If he feels that he cannot reciprocate her sentiment, he

Should he be unable to reciprocate. should give up seeing her. Should she, as some girls of the kind have been known to do, pursue him with letters making appointments, she makes his task of renunciation a difficult one, but he should fulfil it nevertheless.

It is difficult in this way. Suppose a girl writes to a young man : " Meet me at the tea-rooms, No. 440, Bond Street, to-morrow afternoon." There is no chance of replying in time to prevent her going there, and to

"Her ultimate welfare." absent himself would be to administer a severe snub to a girl whom he likes very well, and who has flattered his self-love in many ways during their acquaintanceship. What can he do ? It is a point that he must decide for himself, taking all the circumstances into consideration, and not forgetting to regard her ultimate welfare in the matter at least as much as his own actual wishes.

This may seem to some young men a very " high-falutin' " view to take of such a small matter as meeting a young woman and having tea together. Most of them, finding that a girl was growing fond of them, would

The view of the ordinary young man. encourage the feeling by every means in their power, regardless of whether it could ever end in marriage, and careless of everything beyond the gratification of their own vanity. But there are bright exceptions to these who do not allow themselves to be carried away by the flattery implied in a girl's attentions, and who can consider her welfare in selfless fashion. Sometimes fastidious taste comes to

The manly young man does his own wooing. their aid and makes withdrawal from an interesting companionship comparatively easy. For, after all, the manly young man has a prejudice in favour of doing his own wooing!

It is not at all necessary that a man should accept invitations from a girl to meet her at restaurants, sub-

Invitations from girls. scription dances, bazaars, or any other place. If a girl so far forgets herself, and is so lacking in modesty and propriety as to make appointments with young men in such ways as these, she cannot be worth much, and may lead the young man into a very serious scrape. A public horse-whipping is an extremely disagreeable thing, and yet cases have been known when such have been administered by irate brothers or fathers, when the only fault committed by the young man had been to obey the commands of a forward and bold young woman—one of the sort to whom Hamlet would have said, "Get thee to a nunnery."

Such invitations are better ignored, though it is difficult for the average young man to resist the temptation of being courted and flattered, and of seeking the society of girls who administer these pleasant attentions. But if their standard is a high one, they would say to themselves: "What should I like another fellow to do, supposing the girl were my sister?" (Almost always he mentally adds, "God forbid!") This clears up the question for him at once. If he is high-minded and honourable he keeps away. If he is unscrupulous and self-indulgent he meets the girl and lets the acquaintanceship drift on to dangerous ground.

They are better ignored.

Such girls as these can never tell if a man whose past and present and surrounding circumstances are unknown to her is a scoundrel or otherwise. Fortunately, the code of manners obtaining amongst the educated and well-brought-up forbids all such indiscriminate acquaintance-making. Girls who stoop to it are usually those who have failed to secure attention in their own circle, and belong, as a rule, to the sort of girl who marries a groom or

The danger of the proceeding.

The offenders.

24

runs away with a good-looking foot-man.

A young man once asked me if it would be etiquette to offer an unknown lady an umbrella in the street, supposing she stood in need of one. I replied : "No *lady* would accept the offer from a stranger, and the other sort of person might never return the umbrella." In large towns women of breeding soon learn to view casual attentions from well-dressed men with the deepest distrust. They would suffer any amount of inconvenience rather than accept a favour from a stranger, knowing that so many men make it their amusement to prowl about the streets, looking after pretty faces and graceful figures, and forcing their attentions on the owners. Contemptible curs they are, whether young or old, and they are of all ages. Very young girls have sometimes ex-tremely unpleasant experiences with such men, not only in the streets but in omnibuses, trams, and trains. Culti-vating a gentlemanly exterior, they can yet never be gentlemen, and a good, pure woman finds something hateful in the look of their eyes, the whole ex-pression of their faces. It cannot be denied, however, that there is a corresponding class of women and girls who make promiscuous male acquaintances in the

Offering an unknown lady an umbrella.

A con-temptible class of men.

Their female counterparts.

25

streets, and the young man learns
to distinguish these from respectable
members of the community almost as
soon as the young girl learns to dread
and fear the prowling man. The
existence of such a state of
things makes self-respecting
women most careful to
accept no advances from a
stranger, and the true gentleman, understanding this, refrains from
offers of assistance that he would gladly
make were society so constituted as to
be free from such pests as the above.

Offers of service from strangers not therefore allowable.

In passing ladies on the promenade,
in the street or Park, if a man chance
to be smoking, he always
takes his cigar from his
mouth, replacing it when
the lady or ladies have
passed on. In the crowded streets of
great cities this, if carried out in full
entirety, would be too much. Therefore it is observed only with reference
to such ladies as pass the smoker quite
closely. "I know he is a gentleman,"
said a girl once of a good-looking
young fellow whose appearance had
pleased her—"I know he is a gentleman, for he stopped smoking directly
he saw us." It is in the observance of
little things of this kind that one shows
clearly one's breeding or lack of it.

On removing a cigar when passing a lady.

When a young man is walking with
a lady, and happens to meet another
lady with whom he is on more intimate
terms than with his companion, he must

ask pardon of the latter if he should stop to speak. " Excuse me for one moment," he would say, and his companion, if a gentlewoman, would walk some yards on, and then slowly stroll along until he joined her again. The strict rule is that when walking with a lady a man should never leave her side.

Meeting a more intimate acquaintance when with a lady.

Suppose a young man were to meet his mother or sister while he was in the company of a lady unknown to them, he must not introduce her to them or them to her without having previously obtained special permission on both sides. There are young men who make acquaintance with girls in a lower walk of life than their own. It would be an insult to mother or sister to introduce a milliner's apprentice or an assistant in a shop, or, in fact, any one whom he had picked up without a regular introduction. No respectable young woman would walk with or talk with any man to whom she had not had a proper introduction. The inference is that those who do so are not respectable, and must not, therefore, be introduced to those who are.

The rule for introductions in such a case.

Acquaintance without introduction.

The old rule was that when a gentleman stopped to speak to a lady in the street he walked a little way with her in the direction in which she

Stopping to speak to a lady.

27

had been going. But now this is less observed than it used to be. The lady herself, if she wishes the conversation to be a short one, stops at once, **The old rule and the new.** knowing that it will be easier for a man to terminate it in these circumstances than if he were sauntering by her side.

IN A CARRIAGE.

In handing ladies to their carriage a man offers his right arm to the senior of the party and walks with her to the door, opening it with his left hand. The others will probably follow without escort, but if not, he must offer it to each in turn, holding an umbrella over them should it be raining. He closes the door and conveys their orders to the footman or coachman. Should he be invited to enter the carriage with them, he always takes the back seat—that is, with his back to the horses—unless specially invited to the front one. He must not either raise or lower the windows unless requested to do so. Should he be smoking, he throws away his cigar or cigarette at once. If he should be a very intimate acquaintance of the lady, he may ask her permission to smoke, but never otherwise, since it is disagreeable for a woman to refuse such permission, and consequently she often gives it when she really dislikes the smell of tobacco,

Handing ladies to their carriage.

The man takes the back seat.

On smoking in a carriage.

especially in the limited space of a carriage, should it be a closed one.

It may be as well to mention here that the proper pronunciation of the word "brougham" is as though it were spelled "broom," quite short and monosyllabic. This is a trifle, of course, but, like many another equally small matter, it is indicative of those accustomed to good society.

Pronuncia-tion of "brougham."

IN A HANSOM.

In handing a lady into a hansom care must be taken to protect her dress from the muddy wheel. The gentleman asks if she would like the glasses down, and conveys her instructions to the driver, then raises his hat as she drives away. Should he be accompanying her in the hansom, she seats herself at the nearest side to the pavement, so that when he enters he will not have to go round a corner, as it were. In this case he gives the cabman instructions across the roof of the cab, and if his companion wishes the glasses to be lowered, he asks for them through the trap-door at the top of the cab. He must never smoke when the glasses are let down—to do so would render the atmosphere unbearable to almost any woman. But if he knows his partner in the drive sufficiently well, he can ask permission to smoke, should the glasses not be required.

Guarding the lady's dress.

When accompanying the lady.

SMOKING.

THE etiquette in this, as in many other matters, has quite altered during the last few years. At one time

The domain of Princess Nicotine.

it was considered a sign of infamously bad taste to smoke in the presence of women in any circumstances. But it is now no longer so. So many women smoke themselves, that in some houses even the drawing-room is thrown open to Princess Nicotine. The example of the Prince of Wales has

The leader of the fashion.

been largely instrumental in sweeping away the old restrictions. He smokes almost incessantly. On one occasion, at the Ranelagh Club, I noticed that he consumed four cigars in rapid succession, almost without five minutes' interval between them. The only time that he left off smoking, during the three hours that he remained in the Pavilion with the Princess and other ladies, was for ten minutes when tea was handed round.

It is now no uncommon thing to see a man in evening dress smoking in a brougham with a lady on

The lengths to which a smoker may now go.

their way to opera, theatre, or dinner engagement. This is going rather far, for a woman's evening dress implies shut windows, except in the height of summer, and her garments become as much impregnated with the odour of tobacco as if she had herself been smoking.

Some men have a knack of ridding their clothes and themselves of the fumes of smoke in a wonder-

On getting rid of the smell. ful way. Perhaps one reason of this is that the tobacco they use is of a mild sort.

Perhaps the diligent use of the clothes-brush is another. But there are also men round whom cling the

Try the clothes-brush. odours of stale tobacco with a very disagreeable constancy. Why it should be so I cannot pretend to say. It must be due to carelessness of some kind, and carelessness in such matters amounts to bad manners. Even to men who smoke—and much more to those who do not—the smell of stale tobacco is revolting. Fancy, then, how it must offend the olfactory nerves of women. Such men suggest the stableyard while they are yet several yards away !

A very delicate, even exquisite, personal cleanliness is characteristic of the true gentleman, and more

Personal cleanliness a hall-mark of the English gentleman. particularly the English gentleman, who is noted all the world over for his devotion to his "tub" and his immaculate propriety in all matters of the toilette. This is not claiming too much for my countrymen.

It is acknowledged by other nations that ours is superior in this respect. Once, indeed, I heard a curious inversion of this. At a foreign hotel one waiter said to the other in their mutual language : "What dirty fellows these English must be to want such a lot of washing ! I've carried up four cans of water to No. 47 this morning ! "

Sauntering up the street of a small German town one day, two English ladies saw, a couple of hundred yards away, a party of men standing admiring an ancient gateway. "They must be English," said one of the ladies ; and before she could finish her sentence the other finished it for her in the very words she had been about to utter : " They are so beautifully clean ! "

"They must be English."

This characteristic is carried to an extreme in the close clipping of the hair ; but as fashion ordains that it must be worn very short, its behests must be obeyed by all who wish to be in society and of it. "Who is that long-haired fellow ? " is the question invariably asked about any man whose visits to the barber are infrequent. " Must be an artist or a music man," is the frequent commentary. Sometimes he is merely careless of conventionalities, and by being so proves that he is rather " out of it" where good society is concerned. The rule appears

The close-cropped head.

The "long-haired fellow."

to be that directly a man finds that he
has any hair worth brushing, he must
immediately go and have it cut. It
would be much more becoming if
allowed to grow a little longer, but
things being as they are, only the few
can afford to defy the ordinary custom.

IN OR ON AN OMNIBUS.

THE humble omnibus may be thought by some readers too democratic a kind of conveyance to be

The humble omnibus. considered in a book on Manners. Not at all ! There are several reasons why it should have a place in such a volume. The first is, that during the last ten years or so the omnibus has been largely

It is now used by all classes. used by women of the educated, cultured, and well-dressed classes. Another and stronger reason is that no considerations of the kind should affect a man's manners. If he can behave like a gentleman in a carriage, he is almost certain to do so in an omnibus, and *vice versâ*. It is even more difficult in the humbler vehicle. In a carriage one

A fine field for true courtesy. is seldom crowded up to the degree that often occurs in the plebeian " 'bus." In fact, there are far more opportunities for the display of good manners in the latter than in the former. Many of them are of a negative character. True courtesy, for instance, will prevent a man from infringing the rights of his neighbours on either side by occupying more than his own allotted space. Very stout men are obliged to do so, but at least they need not spread out their knees in a way that is calcu- lated to aggravate the evil.

The man who wants all the room.

Nor need they arrange them- selves in a comfortable oblique position, with the result of enhancing the inconvenience they must necessarily cause to those near them. Even a thin man can take up a quantity of room by thus dis- posing himself at an angle of forty-five with the other occupants of an omnibus.

The morning paper may be converted into an offensive weapon in the hands of the rude and careless, who open it out to its fullest width, re- gardless of the comfort of those sitting next them.

The "news- paper" offender.

Newspapers are rather un- wieldy things to turn and twist about in a limited space, but this very circum- stance affords a man an opportunity of displaying his skill in manipulating the large, wide sheets, without dashing them in the face of his nearest neigh- bour, or knocking up against anybody in a series of awkward movements that a little care could easily convert into leisurely, graceful ones.

There is another way in which men are apt to be careless, and that is in the disposal of a wet umbrella. Women are even more so, but these remarks are in- tended particularly for men, and beyond acknowledging that nem-

The wet umbrella nuisance.

bers of my own sex are equal sinners,
I must leave them out of the question.
When any one takes a dripping umbrella
into an omnibus, he must charge himself with the task of seeing that it
annoys no one but himself. If he can,
at the same time, protect himself, well
and good ; but he must be altruistic in
the matter and care for others first ;
the alternative being to prove himself
lacking in one form of good manners.
He must not even let his wet umbrella
lean up against a vacant part
The rights of of the cushioned seat, render-
the absent. ing it damp for the next
comer. His social conscience cannot
be up to its work if he permits himself
to ignore the right of the absent to
consideration, merely because they are
absent.

Allowing umbrellas and sticks to
protrude so as to trip up unwary
passengers is another thing
Carrying to be avoided. Carrying a
umbrellas and stick or umbrella under the
sticks. arm with the ferule protrud-
ing at the back and threatening the
eyes of those who walk behind, is
always a reprehensible practice, and
one that is fraught with danger, and it
is perhaps more than ever dangerous
when the proprietor is ascending or
descending the steps of an omnibus.
At such moments passengers are liable
to sudden checks from various causes,
and the resultant backward jerk can be
quite annoying enough to those behind

without the aggravation of a pointed stick assaulting them. I have seen a girl's hat torn off her head in this way, its numerous securing pins making havoc in her coiffure and eliciting lively expressions of pain.

It might appear hardly necessary to advocate care in walking up past other passengers inside an omnibus, for fear of treading on their feet, and to recommend a word of apology in case of any such transgression. But there have been cases which point to the desirability of a word of advice on such points.

Entering and leaving an omnibus.

Apology covers a multitude of social sins.

The ready apology covers a multitude of social sins. From some men it comes with an expression of such earnest solicitude that, anxious to reassure them, one quite willingly makes light of the damage done

In escorting a lady a man hands her into the omnibus before entering it himself ; and if she prefers the top, he lets her mount the staircase in front of him. There seems to be an idea in the lowly classes that it is correct to precede a lady in ascending steps or stairs. This is not in accordance with the practice of good society. If circumstances do not admit of the two walking abreast, then the lady goes first, both in ascending and descending any stairs.

The lady first, entering and leaving.

It is by no means necessary that any

39

man should resign his seat in or on an omnibus simply because a woman wishes for it. The conductor has no right to ask "if any gentleman will go outside to oblige a lady"; and no gentlewoman would allow him to ask such a favour on her behalf. The inside passengers have selected inside seats, thereby testifying to their preference for them, and they should be allowed to retain them without interference. I have seen a delicate-looking boy, racked with a hacking cough, induced to ride outside on a cold and rainy night in order that a fat, rosy, healthy woman might have his inside seat. I felt all the more indignant on his behalf because the woman never even thanked him. It was no business of mine, but I was rejoiced to hear a man's voice mutter in the darkness, "She looks better able to face it than that pale-faced lad." But the woman wore a smug, well-pleased air, little knowing that her fellow-passengers were almost all regarding her with a feeling of dislike.

I repeat that no lady, in the highest sense of the term, would ever permit the conductor of an omnibus to ask such a favour for her. She would not ask it for herself; unlike a woman whom I saw, one day, mount on the step of an omnibus and inquire of the

On giving up one's seat to a lady.

Women offenders.

No lady would request this favour.

"insides," " Won't any genelman ride outside to oblige a lydy ?" the "ly-ly" being herself.

It can never be out of place for a man to give up his seat in favour of the old and infirm, or for a woman with a baby in her arms. But such matters as these belong to a region of heart and mind beyond mere manners, and it is useless to suggest any line of action on such subjects. The impulse must come from within.

Higher laws than etiquette.

There have been women so unreasonable as to complain of men smoking on the top of an omnibus. Could anything be more illogical? First, they invade the seats that have been claimed by man as his right (though perhaps unjustly) for many long years, and then they feel annoyed because he smokes in their presence. Or, to speak accurately, they are petulant because his tobacco is often rank, strong, and consequently evil-smelling. But no man need feel it necessary to put out his pipe or throw away his cigar in these circumstances. Should he find himself so placed that the wind blows his smoke in the face of a woman he may propose to change seats with her, in order that she may be spared the inconvenience. But no woman could rationally expect him to do more.

Smoking on the top of an omnibus.

A man is justified in so doing.

41

ON HORSEBACK.

A GREAT change has taken place during the last few years in the character of riding costume for the Park.

Riding costume for the Park. The subject may scarcely be a suitable one for a little book intended for those unaccustomed to the usages of the society of the wealthy. But there are almost always exceptional cases in which such information may be found of use. Only quite old-fashioned people ride in black coats,

Disappearance of the black coat. the usual gear consisting of knickerbocker suits with Norfolk, or other country jacket, brown tops and bowler hats. It must be admitted that this is a distinct gain in picturesqueness. Straw hats are often seen on riders in the Park, but these have not quite so good an effect. The old formalities in dress are rapidly disappearing. A man may

The scope and limitations of the tweed suit. ride in town in a tweed suit, which once would have been considered highly heterodox. He may even walk about London in the height of the season in a tweed suit, but it is not considered correct for him to join his friends in the Park without reverting to the black coat and high hat. Many an old statesman is still to be seen in the Park riding in frock-coat and tall hat, just as John Leech depicted the men of his day.

There are certain rules of etiquette connected with riding on horseback, which no one can afford to ignore. It is extremely ill-mannered to gallop noisily past a mounted lady, the risk being of startling her horse and inconveniencing her, if not subjecting her to an accident. The rule of the road for equestrians is to keep to the *The rule of the road for equestrians.* left, exactly the opposite to that for pedestrians. In passing others in front a detour is made to the right; in meeting other riders or wheel traffic of any sort the rider keeps close to the left. In accompanying a lady the gentleman keeps on her right hand, whether in town or on country roads.

At a meet of hounds, *At a meet of hounds.* where ladies in carriages often assemble, it is not polite to keep too near them if mounted on a fidgety horse. When the hounds throw off, the inexperienced in such matters has a disagreeable way of getting in front in his eager- *"A crime of the blackest dye."* ness, and sometimes over-riding the hounds. This, in the eyes of the huntsman, is not a fault; it is a crime of the blackest dye. If commissioned to take charge of a lady in the hunting-field a man

43

MANNERS FOR MEN.

must sacrifice his sporting instincts to
a certain extent in order to see her
safe over her fences, giving
A man's duty to his charge. her a lead, or following her
lead as circumstances may
dictate. His desire to be in at the
death may be as great as hers, but he
must not indulge it at the expense of
his politeness. Very often his charge
may beg of him to go on and leave her
to her own devices. If he should perceive that she is really uncomfortable
about keeping him back he
His responsi-bility ends only with the hunt. may possibly yield to her
persuasion, but in the case
of any accident happening
to her he would be certainly called to
account by those who had placed her
in his charge.

One of the mistakes made by novices
in the hunting-field is that of getting
themselves up in "pink,"
A common error. though they may not be a
member of any hunt. This
is more particularly the case when the
packs are near town. Good West End
tailors would never allow their clients
to make such mistakes as these. They
are the best authorities on all the
minutiæ of country riding
Advice to the novice. costume, and it is well for
the customer to put himself
unreservedly in the hands of the long-
experienced in such matters. Of course
this means high charges. Experience
and skill are commercial commodities,
just as much as fine cloth and silk linings,

44

but if a man can afford to go a-hunting he ought to be able to afford the adv ce of a good tailor.

In mounting a lady on horseback the gentleman takes her left foot in his right hand, and when she springs he helps her in this manner to reach the saddle, afterwards adjusting her left foot in the stirrup and arranging her habit for her.

Assisting a lady to her mount.

DRIVING.

THE same rule of the road applies to driving as to riding. In the crowded traffic of large towns and "Keep to your left." cities it would be difficult, if not impossible, to observe the good old rule of courtesy that prohibits the driver of any private carriage from overtaking and passing that of a friend or neighbour on the road. The members of the Four-in-Hand and Coaching Clubs still observe it, and seldom pass each other without an apologetic wave of the hand or raising of the hat. A gentleman driving a mail phaeton in the Park with a lady by his side must, of course, Acknowledging salutes. acknowledge all salutes by raising his hat, if he is sufficiently expert to admit of his doing so without risk. It is not every one who can emulate the Prince of Wales, who, when driving a coach, can take a cigar from his lips and raise his hat with the whip-hand, the reins, of course, being in the left. It is not unusual, nowadays, to see a man Handing a lady up to her coach seat. driven by a lady. In such a case he must be on the alert to afford her every assistance in his power. In handing

46

a lady up to her place on a coach some expertness is required, especially where the usual short ladder is not available, and she has to mount first on the wheel and then on to the coach itself.

The box-seat of a coach to the left of the driver is considered the place of honour, and the lady invited to occupy it is very appreciative, as a rule, of this mark of attention. It is scarcely necessary to remark that a **Invitations to coach drives.** man must be as careful about the invitations for a drive on his four-in-hand as he would be in other circumstances. A lady would resent being asked to meet any one unsuitable in a drive, even though the latter may be relegated to a back seat. Sometimes ladies are very anxious to take the reins and drive themselves, a circumstance which has often occasioned agonies of nervousness to other women on the coach. It is quite **A man may refuse a lady the coach reins.** possible to refuse such a request in a polite and gentlemanly way, partly by seeming to ignore it or laughing it off. It is not a bad plan when some such request is supposed to be imminent to bind oneself beforehand by a promise to one of the timid **On dismounting, when calling for a lady.** ladies. This promise can be produced with great effect when occasion arises. A man usually dismounts when calling for a lady to take her for a ride,

47

if she is to be mounted. Sometimes, however, this rule is remitted, as in the case of a restive and very fresh animal ; the groom then assists the lady to mount. The driver of a four-in-hand very seldom dismounts in such circumstances, though, of course, there are exceptions to this as to almost all other rules.

It used to be considered bad manners to smoke when driving with a lady. This is now quite antedilu-
On smoking when driving. vian, so to speak. Permission must, of course, always be asked of the lady. It is scarcely ever refused, and it is almost an exceptional thing to see a man driving without a cigar between his teeth.

Should the lady driven meet some acquaintances unknown to her charioteer, and wish to stop and converse with them, he raises his hat and awaits her pleasure. She will probably introduce him, but if not he takes no part in the conversation. The only thing he can do is to remain passive, but unless the lady feels justified in introducing him it is an error of taste on her part to enter into conversation with her friends.

Some ladies have a great disinclination to mount a four-in-hand or mail phaeton until the driver is
In which case the rule may be broken. seated with the reins in his hand and in full command of the horses. There is nothing surprising in this, for, after all, the groom who stands at the head of

the horses before the start has very
little control over them, and one or two
disagreeable accidents have occurred in
this way, the horses taking fright and
escaping from his grasp.   Consequently
it would be no breach of good manners
for the gentleman driving to take his
seat and thus reassure his nervous
companion.

GAMES AND RECREATIONS.

A MAN who can play a good game of chess, or even an excellent rubber of whist, must be aware that the acquirement involves an education in itself. Neither is ever likely to become unpopular among the best classes of society. Chess and whist clubs increase in number as time goes on ; but for the purposes of everyday life less exigent games are found more useful. Billiards, backgammon, poker, bézique, baccarat, écarté, draughts, vingt-et-un, and loo may be mentioned among the minor accomplishments with which the modern young man finds it convenient to be equipped. That a bad use has been made of some of these by converting them into media for gambling is not to be denied. At the same time there is no reason why those who play them in moderation should refrain from doing so because others abuse rather than use these means of recreation. A round game affords a very innocent mode of spending an enjoyable evening, and country-house life especially is often

Chess and whist permanently popular.

One should be able to play the minor games.

These things are innocent in themselves.

enlivened in this way. Home life, whether in town or country, is apt to become monotonous, particularly for the young members of the

And often quite necessary. family, if there is not occasionally an amusing game got up to pass away the evening hours, and anything that adds to the attractions of home must at least have one excellent recommendation.

Apart from other considerations, the demeanour of a young man when playing cards affords a very

A man's breeding is shown in his play. good test of his manners. Some of them appear to think that the only fun to be had out of the game lies in cheating —very open and transparent cheating, to be sure—but still sufficient to spoil the amusement of others. A curious development of money greed is sometimes observable in players, who will show extreme exasperation at the loss of so simple a coin as a penny.

Irritability over games. There are many fairly good-tempered men (and women) who evince extreme irritability over games of any kind. To play with such as these is very disagreeable, and the tendency to irascibility should be firmly checked by those who wish to be popular in society.

The host or hostess always takes the lead in these games, or else deputes some one else to do so. It is a sign of ill-breeding when any outsider assumes the command of a game without having been asked to do so.

An outsider may not take the lead unsolicited.

Unfortunately, gambling games are very popular at some houses, and it is possible for a young man, being unaware of the fact, to be drawn in and lose more than he can afford before he can politely extricate himself. In such circumstances the only thing he can do is religiously to avoid any such house in future.

Men and houses to be avoided.

It is a matter of notoriety that there are men who make good incomes by fleecing the young and inexperienced whom they invite to their houses under the guise of friendship ; but even when there is no deliberate dishonesty in question, as in these cases, the host or hostess, out of pure love of gambling, draws in the guests to play for high sums. Unpardonable, it is true, but such things have to be reckoned with, and avoided, if possible.

Things to be reckoned with.

The matter is not confined to London ; country-house life has much to answer for under the same heading.

RULE OF THE ROAD ON THE RIVER.

THERE is a rule of the road for the river, and those who boat on the Thames on crowded days fervently wish that it were better understood. There does not appear to be any means of acquiring the necessary information. If such means exist they have never come under my notice, and, for at least one summer, I spent many hours daily in that agreeable form of exercise. Boats coming down with the tide keep the middle of the river; those going against it hug the shore on either side, but in passing other boats coming in the same direction they must go out in a semicircle, leaving the front boat the shore. Tow-boats are always given this advantage. In meeting other boats coming down-stream which really have no right to the shore, but are mistakenly kept near the margin by inexperienced steerers, the boat going up-stream should not go out, but keep towards the land,

The rule of the road on the river.

With the tide—the middle of the stream.

Up-stream—either shore.

The rights of anglers.

The rights of the numerous anglers should be respected ; and it is not only courteous but politic to do so, as it is disagreeable to have the lines entangled in the boat. Row-boats give way to sailing-boats on the Sailing-boats. river, especially when the latter are tacking to use the breeze. As to steam-launches, their motto too often appears to be that " Might is right." Occupants of small boats keep a sharp look-out for these.

In passing through the locks the usual politeness of refraining from shooting ahead of boats in front should be observed. Passing through locks. Any active emulation of this kind is a very risky business in the same way when pulling a boat over the rollers. A man is bound to yield the *pas* to ladies or to any boat containing ladies. In fact, the courtesies of the river may be summed up as similar to those on land.

DINNER-PARTIES.

"MRS. X. requests the pleasure of Mr.
L.'s company at dinner on
Thursday, the 16th of Feb-
ruary, at eight o'clock."

Invitation.

"Mr. L. accepts with pleasure Mrs.
X.'s kind invitation to dinner on Thursday, the 16th
of February."

Acceptance.

These are the preliminaries; the
lady's address being on the sheet
of paper or card on which
her invitation has been
written. Three weeks'
notice is usual, but sometimes, in the
season, when many parties are going
on, invitations are sent out
four, five, or six weeks
beforehand, in order to
secure the guests. In the case of
"lions" even longer invitations have
been given; but as one of the first
principles of good breeding is never
to "corner" anybody, it is scarcely
fair to invite those who
are in much request with-
out giving them the option
of refusal. An invitation of seven or

*Address of
the hostess.*

*The usual
interval.*

*Unfairly long
invitations.*

55

eight weeks' length scarcely allows one to plead a pre-engagement, and often defeats the eager hostess's own end by inducing the "lion" to accept without any intention of being present, writing later on to "renage," to use a good old whist term.

But as our young man is scarcely yet a "lion," and probably not over-burdened with engagements for dinner or any other social function, we may imagine him accepting with a free mind. Should anything intervene to prevent him carrying out his engagement, he is in duty bound to let his **Breaking the engagement.** hostess know as early as possible that he cannot be present at her dinner-party. This is more especially and particularly necessary with dinners, though it holds good with regard to all invitations. But with dinner there is a peculiar obligation laid **Peculiar obligation of the diner-out.** upon the guests. The choice and arrangement of them involves care on the part of the dinner-giver, more so than in the case of any other meal. In fact, dinner stands alone as an institution sacred to the highest rites of hospitality. To be invited is an honour to the young man who is just beginning his social life. To absent himself would be a gross rudeness, unless he could plead circumstances of a pressing nature. It is considered a great infraction of good manners to wire on the very day of the party that one cannot dine as arranged, unless something has occurred to justify such conduct. The hostess can with difficulty find a substitute at short notice, and the whole plan of her table is destroyed by the absence of one person. There are few people who would not feel offended at being invited to fill a gap of the kind, and this is what makes it so extremely discourteous to disappoint at the last moment, as it were. The unfortunate hostess thinks, " Is there any one good-natured enough to come and fill the vacant place ? " Sometimes this is the *raison d'être* of a young man's first invitation. Let him accept it by all means, even though he is perfectly aware that he was not his entertainer's first choice.

On declining at the last moment.

A " fill-up " invitation.

Many a young man feels nervous about his first dinner-party. There are a few puzzling things that trouble him in prospect. He wonders if he should wear gloves, as ladies do, taking them off at the dinner-table. Let me set his mind at rest on this small point, at once. He need not wear gloves. In fact, he must not. Another little matter to be remembered is that a quarter of an hour's grace is always understood in dinner invitations. Should the hour

One's first dinner-party.

Gloves not worn by men.

indicated be 8 o'clock, then care must
be taken to time the arrival at five or
ten minutes past the hour. But it is
better to be too early than too late. A
Punctuality want of punctuality at this
imperative. meal is unpardonable. It is
the very height of rudeness,
annoying to the host and hostess, dis-
pleasing to the guests, and regarded as
outrageous by the cook.

When our young man is shown into
the drawing-room, he at once goes up
to his hostess, no matter
One's first whether there is any one he
duty to one's knows nearer to the door
hostess. than the lady of the house.
This is always a fixed rule, whether it be
on the occasion of a call or visit, or on
having been invited to a party of any
kind. When he has been greeted by
his hostess he looks round the room to
see if there is any one present
Then whom he knows. If so, he
acquaint- goes up to the ladies first, if
ances. there are any of his acquaintance present, and afterwards greets the
gentlemen. His host will probably have
shaken hands with him immediately
after his wife has done so. He will then
be told what lady he is to take down to
dinner, and be introduced to
Introduction her, if he does not already
to partner. know her. He must bow,
not shake hands, and make small talk
for her during the interval between his
introduction and the announcement of
dinner.

DINNER-PARTIES.

Here is his first real difficulty. To converse with a perfect stranger is always one of the initial social accomplishments to be learned, and it is not at all an easy thing at first. It needs practice. Ninety men out of every hundred offer a remark upon the weather; but unless there has been something very extraordinary going on in the meteorological line, it is better to avoid this subject if possible. A girl at Ascot said to me one lovely day, "That's the eighth man who has informed me that it's a beautiful day." Up came a ninth with the very same observation, and both she and I felt inclined to titter like very schoolgirls It is far better to start with something more original. It is as well to keep the pronoun "I" in the background just at first. If your partner is as nice as she might be, she will soon give you abundant opportunity for talking about yourself.

Making small talk.

If possible, avoid talking about the weather.

The first person singular not a good topic.

By the way, a man must not at his very first dinner-party expect to be given a pretty girl to take down. He may possibly be so fortunate, but those prizes are usually reserved for men of more experience in social life. The young man has probably been invited to make up the necessary number of men, and an un-

The beginner's partner.

married lady of uncertain age or an elderly woman without much claim to consideration will probably fall to his share. However, there is this con-

Compensations.

solation, she will be excellent for practising upon. He would not mind making small mistakes so much as if his partner were a young and charming girl. Nor is the art of making small talk so

The small-talk art not so difficult.

difficult as it would be with a pair of bright and youthful eyes beaming into your own, and confusing you into forgetfulness of all but their own delightful language.

But what to talk about is the puzzle of the moment. I have known a good

A good beginning.

beginning made with some such remark as, "Do you know everybody here?" This leads perhaps to the acquisition of some information as to the other guests. At table there will be more to suggest topics. The floral decorations

Some useful topics.

often lead up to conversation. The colours of the flowers remind one of pictures, and the lady on one's right may be asked if she has been to any exhibitions that may be open. If so, what pictures she liked best. Does she paint? Has she read the novel of the hour? What she thinks of it? Does she bike? At this rate our novice gets on swimmingly, and may safely be left to himself.

DINNER-PARTIES.

I must not omit some small details dealing with the guest on his arrival, and on his way afterwards from the drawing- to the dining-room. The servant who admits him takes his overcoat and hat, either in the hall or in a room set apart for the purpose. Should he be accompanied by a lady he follows her upstairs, and she enters the room slightly in advance of him, probably about a yard or so. The young man must not have the appearance of hanging back, however. He walks steadily and rather briskly up the room.

A few details.

On arrival.

The lady precedes her escort.

When the move to the dining-room is made, the gentlemen offer to the ladies the arm which will place them on the wall side of the staircase, thus avoiding the contact of their dresses with the balusters. But should the dining-room be, as it very frequently is, on the same floor as the drawing-room, then the right arm is offered. The lady sits on the right of her escort at table. The servants usually indicate the seats that the guests are to occupy. Sometimes the host, previously instructed by the hostess, comes to the rescue with, "Your seat is here, I believe, Mr. So-and-so," who immediately takes his lady to the chair on the right of the two the couple are to occupy. The system of name-cards

Taking down to dinner.

Positions at table.

is observed in some circles, but it is not a good one. It is distressing, in these days of short sight and small rooms, to see several couples wandering about endeavouring to decipher the names on the small cards. It is much better for the host to have made himself master of the order in which the guests are to be seated, and as he enters the dining-room first with the lady of highest social importance, he is ready to point out their places to each couple as they enter.

Name-cards.

The better plan.

The first thing to be done on sitting down is to unfold the table napkin and place it across the knee. The menu is then consulted, and a mental note made of any favourite dish, so that it may not be refused. But all the time a flow of small talk must be kept up with one's partner of the hour. Sometimes she turns to talk with the man on her right. Then her escort may converse with the lady on his left, if she is disengaged. But he must always remember that his first duty is to her whom he took down.

Preliminaries at table.

There will probably be three or four wineglasses on our young friend's right. One of these—either a long-stemmed, wide-cupped glass or a small tumbler—is for champagne. The coloured glass is for hock, the slenderest and smallest is for sherry,

The wine-glasses.

and the claret-glass occupies in dimensions a midway between those of the champagne and claret glass.

With regard to the knives and forks, everything is now made very easy for the novice by the way in which the table is laid. The tablespoon is for soup, which must be eaten from the side of the spoon close to the point. The fish knife and fork are placed outside the others, so as to be ready to the hand, the fish course coming directly after the soup. The dishes are usually all handed round at dinner-parties, the carving being done at the sideboard or in an immediately adjoining room, but sometimes the host carves the joint and game.

Knives and forks.

Taking soup.

Carving.

There is occasionally a subtle reason for this preference, not wholly unconnected with a taste for those morsels that especially appeal to the gourmand. The host may desire to secure these for some special, appreciative guest—or for himself ! In some families the principal dishes are always placed before the master of the house to be carved. Maidservants can rarely carve well, and butlers have gone considerably out of fashion in the upper middle classes of society of late years.

When offered the usual choice of dishes or wines, the guest must decide at once and indicate his choice without delay. Any hesitation gives him the air of being unable to reject either ; of being in the position, with regard to food, occupied by the poet who wrote—

Choice of dishes and wines.

" How happy could I be with either,
Were t'other dear charmer away ! "

So he must be prompt, and, should the dish be handed round, help himself without delay.

On this very point of helping himself I have seen young men endure excruciating agonies of shyness. Sometimes they take the merest morsel of some excellent dish, though they would like very well to have some more. At other times they help themselves to far too much, because they are so confused that they will not take the necessary time to separate for their own share a moderate quantity. Occasionally they drop the spoon or fork with a clatter into the dish, after which they look intensely miserable for ten minutes or so.

Helping oneself.

The best way to avoid all this is to preserve absolute self-possession by reflecting that the other guests are all too well occupied to pay any attention to such trifling matters. The self-consciousness of which shyness is the outward and visible sign, makes a young man feel that every one is observing him, especially when he is awkward in handling

A useful reflection.

things. But he may console himself
with the conviction that he is of much
less importance to them than their
own dinner, to say nothing of the
ladies who sit beside them.

When asked to choose between
claret or hock, he may either mention
one or indicate the glass.
The order of the wines. "Sherry, sir," is the first
wine handed round. Then
comes the choice between claret and
hock. Afterwards " champagne, sir ? "
Indicating. usually answered by slightly
drawing the champagne-glass
forward, or by a nod ; sometimes by
a shake of the head. An occasional
" Thanks " to the servant is
Thanking servants. not amiss, but it is unnecessary to keep on expressing
gratitude. Some people never dream
of saying "Thank you." Others say it
out of pure graciousness of manner and
gentleness of mind. So our young
man may take his choice.

I have observed that when a neat
and pretty parlourmaid waits at table
Maid-servants at table. she is more likely to be
thanked than a manservant ;
and this not only by gentlemen, but by ladies as well.
I offer no explanation of why this
should be so. I merely record the
fact as I have noted it.

The perfection of service resolves
itself into absolute accuracy of ma-
chinery united to the observant watch-
fulness of long training. One barely

6

discovers that one needs bread when
it is presented at one's elbow. In
the same way, vegetables,
The
perfection of
service.
wine, aërated waters, or
whatever one may be drinking, arrives at exactly the
right moment. The mechanism or
organisation of such waiting is so good
that there is no interruption of conversation. The servants understand that
a mere turning away from the dish
means rejection. Should any guest
find a difficulty in helping himself,
they simplify matters for him as much
as possible.

As the dishes are not named when
they are handed round, it is necessary
to study the menu in order
Studying the
menu.
to know what they are.
Some young people appear
to think that it looks "greedy" to pay
much attention to the information
given on the dainty little bill of fare ;
but this, of course, is one of youth's
delusions. I have seen a short-sighted
young man straining his eyes in the
endeavour to read furtively the names
of the dishes on his menu. He would
have done far better if he had boldly
taken it up in his hand to examine it.

However hungry one may be, the
duty of keeping up a conversation
must not be neglected. The
A topic to be
avoided.
viands must never be chosen
as a topic, for either praise
or blame. If one knows a girl very
well, one may ask, " Do you like

sweets?" or some such question, but it is safer with strangers to avoid the subject of the food provided.

It is scarcely necessary to remark that drinking too much wine is a very bad phase of ill manners. **Moderation in wines.** At one time it was actually fashionable to become intoxicated after dinner, but those days are gone, I am thankful to say. The young man who exceeds in this way is soon made aware of the fact that he has given his hostess dire offence. He is never invited again, or not for a long time.

The wineglass is never drained at a draught in polite society ; nor is it considered polite to eat very quickly.

The knife, fork, and spoon are handled as noiselessly as possible. **As little noise as possible.** Scraping the edge of the knife against the plate is unpardonable. It produces a grating noise that is excessively unpleasant. In sending a plate away to be replenished, the diner leaves his knife and fork or his spoon as the case may be, upon it.

In dealing with bread, use neither knife nor fork. It must be broken with the fingers. There is **Bread must be broken** a story of an absent-minded and short-sighted prelate who, with the remark, "My bread. I think?" dug his fork into the white hand of a lady who sat beside him. He had been badly brought up, or he would not have used his fork, and the white hand would have experienced nothing worse than a sudden grasp.

It requires some expertness and practice for a man with a moustache to take soup in a perfectly inoffensive manner. The accomplishment is worth some trouble.

The moustache and soup.

Some men, who should know better (and some women, too), forget that the mouth should be kept closed while mastication is going on. This is a very important matter. Nature teaches us to keep the mouth open, as any one may see from the way in which children and uncultivated persons eat, but good manners enjoin upon us that to adopt the natural mode is to disgust and annoy those with whom we sit at meat. If these little things have not been learned in childhood, it is difficult to master them afterwards. Mothers should also teach their boys (and girls) never to speak while food is in the mouth, and never to drink until it is quite empty. Who would not be mortified if he were to choke ignominiously at the dinner-table ?

The mouth.

Nature not a good guide in this matter.

The correct way to eat a curry is with a spoon and fork ; but this is the only meat dish that is eaten in this way. Sweetbreads and many other entrées are eaten with the fork alone. It is then held in the

How to eat a curry, &c.

right hand. Should a knife be found
necessary it can, of course, be used.
Vegetable entrées are always eaten
with a fork, held in the right hand.
Fish is eaten with a silver (or plated)
knife and fork. Sauces are never
taken very plentifully. The sauce
ladle, filled, will be generally
sufficient. I once saw a man,
in helping himself to oyster
sauce, look scrutinisingly in the sauce-
boat and carefully fish about for as
many oysters as he could collect in
the ladle. This caused some covert
amusement, except, perhaps, to the last
persons to whom the sauce was handed.
They probably found few oysters.

Taking Sauces.

Bread, biscuits, olives, asparagus,
celery, and bonbons are the forms of
food that may be touched
with the fingers. There used
once to be a rule that a bone
might be picked, if only the
finger and thumb were used in holding
it. But that was in the days when
table cutlery was far from having been
brought to its present condition of
perfection. There is now no excuse
for handling bones—knives and forks
suffice ; and it is only in the lowest
grades of society that they are found
inadequate.

Foods touched with the fingers.

In helping oneself to salad, it must
be placed on the crescent-shaped plate
laid down for that purpose
before it is handed round.
This plate is put at the left side of the

Salads.

round plate. Both knife and fork are
often necessary with salads, but if they
are sent to table as they should be,
with the lettuce and other vegetables
broken small, the fork is quite sufficient. It is always disagreeable to see
a steel knife used with vinegar, and it
should be avoided whenever possible
to do so. Oysters served on the shell

Oysters. are eaten with a fish-knife
and fork. Other fish hors
d'œuvres are eaten with a fish-fork.
It is not always possible to tell, either
from the appearance or name of the
hors d'œuvre, whether it consists of fish
or meat. In that case it is

Hors d'œuvres. safer to use an ordinary fork ;
and for this reason : the fish-
knife has been laid for a fish course,
and if it should have been previously un-
necessarily used for the hors d'œuvre,
it will be needful for the servant to
bring another. Fish rissoles may be
eaten with a fish-fork only—in fact,
any preparation that does not need
the knife.

It is a safe rule never to use either

A safe rule. knife or spoon if the fork
will do. With ice-pudding
or ices in any form a small spoon is
used.

Now let us take the dinner from the
very beginning, and go through the

The courses seriatim. courses. First, there may
be hors d'œuvres, small
morsels of various kinds
which are found ready to hand when

70

the guests sit down. I have already referred to these. Next

Hors d'œuvres.

comes soup, generally one thick and one clear. The attendant offers the diner a choice, and he must promptly make it.

Soup.

When it is set before him he begins at once, not waiting till every one is served. He takes up the tablespoon, placed ready at his right hand, and it is not considered very good form to immediately put some salt into the soup

Taste before salting.

before tasting it. People who pride themselves on the possession of a clever cook sometimes feel annoyed at the distrust of her powers shown in this simple action.

With soup small addenda are often handed. The guest helps himself to these, whether they are

The addenda to soup.

croûtons, fried bread-crumbs or other supplementary provision, with the spoon handed round on the dish.

It is a very old-fashioned piece of good manners to wait till every one is served. So old-fashioned is

When to begin dining.

it that it survives at present only among the uncultured classes. The correct thing to do nowadays is to begin eating without reference to others. The old style must not only have been trying in consequence of seeing one's food grow cold before one's eyes, but it must also have been responsible for making dinner a very slow and tedious meal. Now the attendants remove the plates from the guests first helped directly the fork is laid down, and this greatly accelerates the service.

The soup-plate, if tilted at all, is raised at the side nearest the eater, so that the soup collects at the **Tilting the soup-plate.** furthest point from him. It is generally unnecessary to tilt the plate, however. But the thing to avoid is passing the left hand round it in a half-embrace and **The direction of the tilt.** tilting it towards the eater. This is highly incorrect; it is also dangerous. The soup has been known to spill on the cloth, and even over the diner.

When the servant is removing your soup-plate he will sometimes ask, "Any more, sir?" to which you **Neither soup nor fish** must reply in the negative. **may be** A shake of the head will **helped twice.** suffice. Soup is never helped twice. Nor is fish. This is the next course. Bread is always eaten with fish. I have already explained that a silver knife and fork are **Fish and fish sauce.** used. The sauce handed is almost invariably accepted. Sometimes the cruet is handed round, containing some sort of condiment suitable to the fish served. It is, of course, a matter of choice whether this be accepted or not.

Very few diners work straight through

a menu without omitting some dishes.

Omitting dishes.

The idea of giving so many is that there may be some to suit all tastes. No one is expected to take of all, though it is quite permissible to do so.

After the soup and fish the entrées are handed round. The dishes are

Entrées.

presented at the left side of the diner, and he helps himself with his right hand, a table-spoon being placed on the dish for that purpose ; or with both hands, using spoon and fork, should the nature of the dish render this necessary.

When slices from a joint, or game, or poultry are handed round, the vege-

Accompaniments to dishes.

tables, gravies, and sauces accompanying them are handed after. It is usual to wait for these etceteras before beginning upon the meat, fowl, venison, or game. For instance, no one would commence upon a slice of roast beef or mutton without potatoes or gravy, nor upon a piece of pheasant without browned bread-crumbs, or bread sauce, or gravy. I say "no one" would do it, but I have seen it done, whether in absence of mind or from pressure of appetite I cannot pretend to say. It is a mistake, however.

Sweets and cheese.

Cheese is handed round after the sweets in order to prepare the palate for the enjoyment of dessert wines. This, at

least, was the original meaning of introducing it at this stage of the meal.

Ice-pudding. But now ice-pudding, when
served, follows it, thus con-
tradictorily re-establishing the reign of
sweets. Savouries are handed round

Savouries. with the cheese course.
These are eaten with a fork.
Even a cheese fondu is eaten with a
fork, though the cook occasionally fails
to bring it to the requisite firmness of
consistency, in which case it looks more
suited to a spoon ; but the fork must

Celery. do. Celery is eaten with
the fingers, like asparagus.
This last-named, by the way, if too
much cooked, and consequently very

Asparagus. soft and unmanageable, may
be eaten with the fork,
but must not be touched with the
knife. And again, should asparagus be
served with the melted butter thrown
over it, it must be eaten with a fork.
It very seldom is so served, but I have
met with this mode in some houses.

Cheese ramequins are eaten with the
fingers. Cheese itself is handed round
on a dish or plate with the

Cheese, how pieces cut ready to one's
served. hand. The diner helps himself with the knife laid ready beside
the pieces of cheese, not with his own
knife. If watercress is handed round,
it is taken up in the fingers

Cheese, how and eaten in the same way.
eaten. Cheese is cut in small pieces
and conveyed to the mouth on a

piece of bread or biscuit. Very few persons continue to eat it in the old-fashioned way by carrying it to the mouth with the knife. I have seen it taken up with the fingers, but as cheese is apt to smell rather strong y it is better to avoid touching it.

With regard to sweets, it is a safe rule to use the fork only when it suffices for the work in hand.

A safe rule with sweets. With tarts, as a rule, both spoon and fork are necessary, especially when there is syrup. Cold tart can often be comfortably eaten with a fork. Jellies and creams are eaten with a fork only ; ice-pudding with an ice-spoon, or, failing that, a teaspoon.

From the moment one has unfolded one's napkin and placed the bread it contained at one's left, there is nothing more to do that concerns the " cover," as the preparation for each diner's convenience is called, until the dessert-plate, with its d'oyley, finger-glass, silver knife and fork—and perhaps ice-plate and spoon in addition—is set down before one. Before the

Placing the dessert knife and fork. ices or dessert are handed round, one must place the dessert-knife and fork at right and left, respectively, of one's plate, and, taking up the finger-glass carefully in one hand, with

D'oyley and finger-glass. the other place the d'oyley on the cloth to the left of one's plate, then setting the finger-glass down upon it. I say "carefully," because these glasses are often of the lightest possible kind, and are occasionally of a costly description. Besides, rough handling might tend to spill the water they contain.

With regard to the dessert fruits, Dessert. &c., there are a few puzzles to be found among them for the inexperienced. Grapes present one of these. They are taken up singly, and afterwards the skin and Grapes. seeds have to be expelled as unobtrusively as possible. It is a matter of great difficulty to accomplish this by any other method than using the hand, therefore this is the accepted custom. The forefinger is Expelling curved above the mouth in skin and a manner which serves to seeds. conceal the ejectment, and the skin and seeds are in this way conveyed to the plate, the fingers being afterwards wiped with the Bananas. napkin. Bananas are peeled with the knife and fork, and the pieces are conveyed to the mouth by means of the fork. Oranges are cut in Oranges. two, then in four, and with the aid of knife and fork the contents of each section are extracted in two or more parts, and carried to the lips on the fork. Apples and pears Apples and are peeled with the knife pears, &c. and fork ; peaches, apricots, and nectarines in the same way.

Strawberries are taken by the stem,

dipped in sugar and cream, and carried to the lips with the fingers.

Strawberries. If the fruit has been picked free of husks and stem, it may be bruised on the plate with sugar and cream, and eaten with a spoon. Preserved ginger is eaten with the knife and fork.

A spoon is necessary with pines, melons, and very juicy strawberries, after they have been prepared with the knife and fork.

Pines and melons.

Nuts are cracked with the nut-crackers, and then extracted by the fingers. With filberts and Brazil nuts the knife and fork are called into requisition in order to free them from skin, but walnuts are too intricate for anything less wonderful in mechanism than the human hand. In view of this, they are sometimes prepared before being sent to table, and of late years they have been sold ready cracked and peeled for this purpose.

Nuts.

Almonds are never sent to table in their shells, so that they present no difficulties to the novice. At dessert they are usually accompanied by raisins, which, like the almonds, are carried to the mouth in the fingers.

Almonds.

Crystallised fruits are cut with the knife and fork, unless they happen to be of a small size, such as cherries. In that

Crystallised fruits.

case they are eaten whole, being carried
to the lips on the fork.

Liqueurs are handed round at dessert, poured out ready into the small
glasses that are called after
them. There is generally
a choice, such as "Chartreuse or
Bénèdictine, sir?" to which it is unnecessary to reply, "Both, please," as
a historic young man did once.

Liqueurs.

The servants often leave the dining-
room when the dessert is placed on the
table, and when this is so, the wine is
passed round from hand to hand, each
gentleman attending first to
the lady he has escorted and
then helping himself before
passing on the decanter, claret jug,
or champagne bottle. The good old
fashion of using silver decanter-stands
has long disappeared, to the detriment
of many a good tablecloth. So has the
genial and hospitable fashion of drinking
wine with one's guests, and they with
each other. But this may be rather a
good thing in the interests of temper-
ance.

*Passing the
wines.*

Apropos to this subject, I may remark
that there is now nothing singular in
drinking nothing but water.
The days are gone when a
man was thought a milksop
because he could not " drink
his bottle," or if he refused wine or
spirits. Should any young man prefer
water, he asks for it when the servants
offer him wine. He is then offered

*The water-
drinker not
singular.*

Apollinaris or distilled water or soda-water, or some other preparation of filtered and distilled water, and may choose some of these in preference to plain water.

Claret is the favourite dessert wine of the day, but port is still seen at some tables, and it is usual to offer champagne, as many prefer to drink only one kind of wine throughout the meal, from start to finish. In fact, this is becoming quite a fashion in some sets. The host provides cigars and cigarettes for his guests, and it would not be necessary or advisable to produce one's own supply.

"One wine" diners.

Cigars and cigarettes.

When the ladies rise to leave the dining-room, the gentleman nearest the door opens the door for them, and stands beside it until they have all passed through, when he closes it after them. However anxious he may be to join them in the drawing-room, he must not do so until the others make a move. Sometimes, if he is very young and rather "out of it" when politics or sport are under discussion, his host says to him, "I'm afraid you are bored. If you would like to join the ladies, don't stand on ceremony." But on the other hand he may dread the ordeal of entering the drawing-room alone, and feel that the safer way is to wait for a convoy. This he must decide for himself.

When the ladies leave the dining-room.

Perhaps his host may wish to talk confidentially with some other guest.

A hint from the host. If he makes this apparent to the younger man, the latter must accept any such intimation as the above, understanding it to be a courteous mode of dismissing him.

The ordinary rule is that the gentlemen join the ladies all together, the

The ordinary rule when rejoining the ladies. man of highest position leaving the dining - room first, the host last. Tea is then carried round in the drawing-room, and the gentlemen take the empty cups from the ladies and put them down in some safe place, out of the way of risk of accident. Should

When a lady sings or plays. any lady sing or play, the gentleman nearest to her escorts her to the piano and helps her to arrange her music, to dispose of her gloves, fan, handkerchief, &c.

It is scarcely etiquette for young men to leave first after a dinner-party. It is

Leaving early. more usual for the elders of the party to make the first move towards departure. But should the young man have an engagement of a pressing kind, such as a promise to escort ladies to a ball, he must withdraw in good time, explaining the position to his hostess.

No one leaves after a dinner-party without saying "Good-night" to his host and hostess. Even in the case of

an early departure, before the gentlemen have left the dining-room, the
guest must visit the drawing-room to
make his adieux, not only to the lady
of the house, but to any others who
may be of his acquaintance. Those
whom he has met for the first time
that evening may be saluted with a
parting bow.

At a formal dinner-party the evening
suit is imperative, with dress-coat,
white or black waistcoat, black
trousers, and white tie. When dining
with friends with whom one is on
terms of familiarity, the dinner-jacket
may be substituted for the coat. Black
ties often take the place of white.
Patent-leather shoes or boots must be
worn. It would be unpardonable to
appear in thick walking - boots or
shoes; and the necessity for immaculately polished footgear has cost the
young man of the present day many
a cab. His varnished shoes must
show no trace of mud or dust. To
tell the truth, he often carries a silk
handkerchief in his pocket wherewith
to obliterate the traces of the latter.

The pocket-handkerchief used with
evening dress must be of white
cambric, and of as good a colour as
one's washerwoman will permit. It
ought to be of fine quality. The hair
must be short and very well brushed.

It used to be the custom to tip the
servants on leaving the house where
one had dined as a guest, but this has

fallen into disuse. There are many men who hand a silver coin to the butler, or footman, or waiting-maid who helps them into their coats, calls up their carriage, or hails a cab for them, seeing them into it, or rendering any other service of a similar kind. This is a matter that each man must decide for himself. It is only necessary to remark that the custom of giving shillings or half-crowns to the servants after a dinner-party no longer reigns ; though there are always good-natured folk who will not let it abso lutely die out.

PUBLIC DINNERS.

THE following information is supplied by a gentleman well-known in the City, and thoroughly *au fait* in such matters.

Public dinners.

" Public dinners may be classed as those given by associations, or public bodies, and those given by institutions, such as some of the great City companies. When given by an association, the function is generally managed by a committee, who have the arrangement of all the details, such as choosing the menu, the wines, preparing the programme of music, instrumental or vocal, and arranging the due sequence of the speeches. A guest invited to such an entertainment who may not be of the few highly placed personages who sit at the cross-table or on the daïs, and from whom speeches are expected, will, on arriving at the hall, hotel, or public institution selected, find that the first thing required of him will be his invitation card. In exchange for this he will be handed a more or less elaborate menu card, which will also contain the list of music

When given by an association.

On arrival.

and a sketch showing the positions of the guests' seats at the tables. After depositing his hat and overcoat in the cloak-room, receiving a numbered ticket for them, he enters the reception- or drawing-room, his name is announced, and he passes into the room, goes up to the members of the com-

Saluting the hosts.

mittee, who stand by themselves to receive the guests, bows or shakes hands, and passes on to join the other guests who are either sitting or standing in groups engaged in conversation. When dinner

When dinner is announced.

is announced the hosts and the highest in rank of the guests file into the dining-room and take up their position by their chairs, followed by the rest; any clergyman present says grace on being asked to do so, and the banquet commences. Strangers sitting next to each other soon fall into conversation, and after the dispatch of the solid portion

The order of the ceremony.

of the repast come the speeches. Music is played at intervals, perhaps a few songs sung by professionals, then dessert, cigars, and coffee, after which the guests find their way to the drawing-room for more general conversation, some preferring to leave without re-entering the drawing-room. In such large gatherings it is not necessary to take leave of their hosts, as a rule.

" Dinners given by City companies are very much on the same principle.

PUBLIC DINNERS.

The guest has but to don his evening clothes and carry himself with easy composure, not always quite a simple matter to the inexperienced, if one may judge from the hurried steps and the sudden bob that many give on entering the reception - room after arrival."

Dinners given by City companies.

At dinners given on behalf of charities, it is well to go prepared with a subscription, as a collection is often made on these occasions. If not prepared to subscribe, it is more discreet to stay away.

Dinners for charities.

With regard to tips the only ones really recognised are those for which the plates on the cloak-room table are laid ready in expectation of small silver coins. Though no fees are actually necessary at table, the initiated person is well aware that the man behind his chair can administer to his wants and see that he is liberally provided with viands and wines or other matters without keeping him waiting longer than necessary. A tip, quietly conveyed before the dinner is under way, is not by any means wasted.

On tips.

It sometimes happens that semi-official dinners are given at private houses, when proprietors of newspapers or wealthy men interested in certain undertakings, entertain the staff of those employed. In such circum-

Semi-official dinners at private houses.

stances it may be as well to warn the
guests against addressing the footmen
as "waiter." This may appear to be
superfluous advice, but I have myself
been present when the mistake was
made, evidently to the intense indig-
nation of the magnificent being thus
addressed.

At such dinners as these, the host
treats his guests as his social equals
for the nonce. By having invited
them to his house he places himself
in the position of regarding them as
he would his own friends at his dinner-
table. Any infraction of this would be
in the worst taste. It is also usual to
abstain from any business talk at such
times as these, the conversation being
encouraged to dwell on general topics.

Though the fiction of social equality
is maintained by the host, the guests
need not adopt a familiar, free-and-
easy manner in response. True manliness involves sufficient self-respect to
preserve the possessor from falling
into this error; but it is, perhaps, a
little difficult for the novice, on such
occasions, to bear himself in such wise
as to avoid undue familiarity on one
hand and an air of stiffness and stand-
offishness on the other. In his anxiety
not to appear to presume upon the
friendliness of his host's manner, he is
apt to wear a rather repellent air.
And this is more particularly so when
the *employé* is by birth the equal, if
not the superior, of his entertainer. It

often happens that a man at the head
of a great business has risen from
obscure beginnings to the command of
wealth and a high position in the
world, enjoying a title and many of
the extraneous advantages of rank.
Among those whom he employs may
be several who are his social superiors
in all but wealth ; but any of them who
imagine that this fact gives them any
claim upon his consideration or en-
titles them to converse with him upon
a footing of equality, make a radical
mistake.   Their position, as regards
their employer, is exactly that justified
by their standing in his firm.   The true
gentleman is well aware of this, and
would never dream of asserting himself in any way on the strength of
being well-born or highly educated.
He leaves all that kind of thing to the
man who feels his claim to gentleman-
hood to be so shadowy and insecure
as to need constant insistance.

Besides, the host is usually the elder,
and deference to seniority is an important part of good manners, and sits
extremely well upon the young.

AT A RESTAURANT.

WHEN accompanying ladies who express a wish for refreshment, it is not necessary to select a very expensive restaurant or confectioner's. One suitable to the social status of the party should be chosen. The young man must pay for what his companions eat and drink, and very often this is a most embarrassing matter. He may have enough money in his pocket to defray the bill, and he may not. In any case, he is often unable to afford it, but the probabilities are that if he has the wherewithal about him, he will pay in order to extricate himself from an awkward predicament, even though he may consequently be crippled financially for some days to come. If he has only two or three shillings in his pocket, he feels extremely uncomfortable. No well-bred woman or girl would ever place an acquaintance on the horns of such a dilemma. But unfortunately there are many girls and

Should ladies request refreshment.

The man pays.

Though he cannot afford it.

No well-bred woman would make the request.

88

women who are lacking in taste and refinement, and who would regard it as an excellent joke to play such a trick upon a "fellow," as they would probably call him, and enjoy his discomfort.

The best thing to do in such a case is to be perfectly frank and open. "I'm extremely sorry, but I have not sufficient cash with me for the purpose." It is very disagreeable to have to say so, but it is less mortifying than to have to acknowledge it to the waiter at the restaurant. A young man told me that he had once, in such a case, to leave the table on pretence of speaking to the proprietor and fly round to a pawnbroker's to pledge his watch.

The best course to adopt.

A really well-bred girl or woman would make it clear that she intended to pay for her own meal, and that only on that condition would she accept the escort of the young man.

A well-bred girl would bear her own expenses.

Sometimes after a run on a bicycle or a hot walk, a young man will say to his sister and her friend, "Come in and have an ice." If the friend is one of the unscrupulous sort, she will very probably run him into what, for him, is a considerable expense. He must pay it, however, and the worst of it is that he cannot sit there and let her eat all by herself. Even his sister, should she be

On taking advantage of a man's generosity.

present, must in good manners join in to a certain extent. Otherwise the implied reproof would be too obvious for good breeding.

AT LUNCH.

LUNCHEON is a comparatively informal meal. The guests do not pair off, as at dinner, but on the meal being announced the host, if there be one, would open the door for the ladies, who would go down-stairs, followed by the hostess, the gentlemen behind her. Very often the master of the house is absent at luncheon, in which case the hostess would rise, and, ad-dressing her principal guest, would propose to her to lead the way downstairs. "Shall we go down to lunch, Mrs. So-and-so?" would be sufficient. The other ladies would probably be sufficiently versed in the laws of society to refrain from preceding those of higher position, and the hostess would always be the last lady to leave the drawing-room. The guests sit down where they please, the host or hostess sometimes making a suggestion on the matter.

Going down to luncheon.

In the absence of the host.

Positions at table.

After the meal the guests return to the drawing-room, but only for a short time. The gentle-men resume their overcoats and take their hats and umbrellas in the

After the meal.

91

hall, where they had left them. Should
a man make a call at lun-
cheon-time, he is often asked
to remain for the meal. In
that case he would carry his
hat and stick into the dining-room with
him, just as he would if making an
ordinary call. But it is much better
never to call anywhere at lunch-time
unless one is on very familiar terms
with the family. Many young men
acquire a reputation for "cadging" for
lunch or dinner in this way.

Making calls at luncheon-time.

Invitations from the younger members of the family are not official,
unless plainly endorsed by
the elders, or one of them.
"Miss Lucy invited me to
lunch" is a poor plea.
"Frank asked me to come and dine
this evening," is no better. Young
men cannot be too particular about
this matter. "I'll get my mother to
ask you to dinner, old man," would be
the safer sort of invitation. The lady
of the house must fix the date, and she
usually writes the invitation herself or
gives it personally.

Invitations from young members of the family.

Should a daughter of the house give
a young man an invitation to any meal,
without reference to her
father or mother, it would
be incorrect in the highest
degree to accept it. As to
children, their invitations go
for nothing, of course, though cases
have been known in which they have

Unendorsed invitations from a daughter of the house.

been accepted. "I met little Eddy in the park, and he made me come in with him." This has a very poor and pitiable sound at luncheon hour or tea-time.

It is not necessary to make one's adieux to each guest in turn. The hostess is taken leave of

Making one's adieux.

first, as a rule, and the lady, or ladies, with whom one has been conversing will expect a special word and bow, perhaps offering a hand; but a general bow will be sufficient for those to whom one is not very well known. It is only at family parties that one has conscientiously to go round the room shaking hands with everybody.

FIVE O'CLOCK TEA AND AFTER-
NOON AT-HOMES.

GENTLEMEN are in great request at
five o'clock tea. Their duties are
rather onerous if there are
Duties of men at five o'clock tea. but one or two men and the
usual crowd of ladies. They
have to carry teacups about,
hand sugar, cream, and cakes or muffins,
and keep up all the time a stream of
small talk, as amusing as they can make
it. They must rise every time a lady
enters or leaves the room, opening the
door for her exit if no one else is
nearer to it, and, if his hostess requests
him, he must see the lady downstairs to
her carriage or cab.

With regard to the viands, a man
helps himself, but not till he has seen
that all the ladies in his
His own refreshment. vicinity have everything
they can possibly want.
His hostess, or some lady deputed by
her to preside at the tea-table, gives
him tea or coffee, and he adds sugar
and cream.

With regard to afternoon at-homes,
the arrangements are quite
Afternoon at-homes. different. Invitations are
sent out a fortnight or
three weeks before, generally the latter,

and in the height of the season even longer.

Suppose the young man's name to be Edward Smith. His invitation would be as follows:—

MR. EDWARD SMITH.

—

LADY DART

AT HOME,

Tuesday, November 3rd.

4 TO 7.

12, Evergreen Square.

R. S. V. P.

He replies, on a sheet of note-paper:—"Mr. Edward Smith has much pleasure in accepting Lady Dart's kind invitation for Tuesday afternoon, November 3rd."

Accepting invitation.

It's a great mistake to write:—"Will have much pleasure in accepting." Accepting is the action of the present moment while he is writing the reply. "Will have" refers to the future, and is therefore unsuitable. The answering of invitations is a simple matter enough, but it is a test of good breeding.

A great mistake.

95

AT THE PLAY.

AT a theatre the underbred man is often in evidence, not only in the low-priced seats, but also all over the house. He has been seen— and heard—in private boxes.

The under-bred man at the play.

A well-known music-hall celebrity administered a scathing reproof to one of these, who persisted in talking loudly while she was singing. Stopping short, she looked up at the box in which he sat, and cried : "One fool at a time, please," after which he was as quiet as a mouse. It is a piece of bad manners to enter the theatre late, disturbing the audience and annoying the players or singers. It is equally rude to leave before the entertainment is ended, unless the interval be chosen when nothing is going on.

Entering late.

At a concert this is particularly true, for there are devotees of music who hang upon every note and to whom it is a distinct loss to miss a single phrase of the compositions they have come to hear. Singers, actors, and actresses generally possess the sensitive, sympathetic, artistic temperament, and it is wounding to them to see

And leaving early.

Inattention uncivil.

members of the audience fidgeting, rustling about, chattering, laughing, and otherwise showing inattention when they are doing their best to entertain them. It is, therefore, uncivil to betray inattention. A little appreciation goes a long way with the members of the professions of music and

On appreciation. the drama. An actor told me once that after having made a certain speech two or three times without any sign of amusement from the audience, on the fourth night of the play a single silvery note of musical mirth was heard from the stalls. It was but one note—say E flat on the treble clef—but the audience immediately joined in, perceiving the point of the speech as though it had been illuminated for them by this one little laugh. He declared that ever after that night his formerly unsuccessful "lines" elicited a roar of laughter. Probably this was partly due to the sense of encouragement he felt, inspiring him to due emphasis.

In taking ladies to a place of entertainment a gentleman hands them into their carriage, a cab, or

In taking ladies to a place of entertainment. an omnibus, getting in last. Arrived at their destination the gentleman alights first, handing out the ladies, and giving any necessary orders to the coachman, or paying the cabman's fare. By the way, it is always as well to give instructions to the coachman about where he is to

8

be found, and at what hour he is to pick up his party, before entering the carriage, as policemen view *Instructions to the coachman.* with much disfavour any prolonged dialogue outside a place of entertainment where vehicles are setting down their occupants in quick succession. Should there be a footman, of course all these difficulties are obviated, as he can carry the instructions to the coachman, and also knows where to find the carriage when the performance is over.

Should a hired brougham be used as a conveyance in going to any place of entertainment, or even a *Should a hired brougham be used.* party at a private house, it is an excellent plan to give the coachman a bright-coloured handkerchief, scarlet or orange perhaps, that he may wear it conspicuously displayed, and can in this way be at once recognised. It is a miserable business on a wet night to *To obviate waiting.* hunt for a brougham up and down ill-lighted streets when in evening dress and patent leather boots, and anything that tends to shorten the task is advisable. Nor do ladies enjoy waiting in the draughty vestibule of opera-house, theatre, or concert-room for an indefinite period while a short-sighted cavalier is groping about the streets for their carriage.

If it is a question of a cab, the commissionaire at the door is the best person to get one, which he will do for a small fee.

Here again a word of warning is needed. There are men who, in their special care of the ladies in their charge, forget that it is no part of the duty of a gentleman to ignore the claims of other women who have not the advantage of belonging to their party. I have seen men who ought to have known better rudely pushing other ladies away from the door of a cab or railway carriage in order that their own womenkind may be well looked after. It is all very well to be attentive and anxious to do one's best, but it is ill-bred to the last degree to subject to rudeness any ladies who happen to be without a gentleman to look after them.

A word of warning.

Consideration due to all women.

Retribution followed very swiftly in one instance of the kind. At Sandown station one day the second special train for Waterloo was coming in, and the platform was crowded with gaily-dressed women, tired and hot after the walk across the fields on a tropical July day. A lady and small Eton boy were together, and suddenly, when about to open the door of a carriage at the moment the train came to a standstill, found themselves all but thrown down by a sweeping motion of the arm of a young man who was bent on reserving that particular carriage for his party. With

An instance.

out a word of apology to the lady, he
shouted to his sisters and friends to
" Come on," still holding back the two
who had wished to get in. They
entered the next compartment, and as
they did so the lady remarked to her
companion, " What an extremely ill-
mannered person that is ! " Meanwhile
the party next door were settling down
and congratulating themselves on having
secured seats, when one of them turned
to their over-zealous friend and remarked, " I saw Lady Blank get into
the next carriage with her eldest boy."
" *Who ?* " he asked, with a sudden and
remarkable rush of colour on his face.
The lady to whom he had behaved so
rudely turned out to be one from whom
he had that very morning received a
long-desired invitation to spend a few
days at her country house in the
following month. This he owed to
the good offices of a friend in the
F. O., and, delighted at having made
such a step in his social career, he had
at once written off accepting the invitation. It is scarcely necessary to add
that he never made the visit, but had
to wire at the last moment one of those
conventional excuses that the " unco
guid " call fibs, but which are only the
transparent devices adopted by society
to lubricate some of the more difficult
of its processes.

Between the acts of a play the
modern man thinks it his duty to
himself to go out and have a drink,

AT THE PLAY.

perhaps smoke a cigarette. There was
a time when, had any such suggestion

The interval. been made to a gentleman
who had constituted him-
self the escort of a lady, he would
have asked, though perhaps not in
Milton's words—

"And leave thy fair side all unguarded, lacy?"

But now the majority of young men
visit the bar or the *foyer*. But who
shall say what golden opinions are won
by those who do not follow the custom,
who refrain from acquiring the odour

of tobacco, or whiskey, or
How a man may win golden opinions. brandy while they are in
the company of ladies in
the heated atmosphere of a
theatre? A lady sometimes says to
the men of her party, "I see that there
is a general stampede going on. Don't
mind me if you would like to go out."
If they go she thinks, "Oh, they are
just like the rest." If they stay she
says to her own heart, "How delightful it is to find a man who can do
without a B.-and-S. or a smoke for
two or three hours!" and up he goes
many pegs in her estimation.

Apart from the lady he is with and
considerations connected with her,

there is the inconvenience
Other considerations. to which many of the
audience are subjected by
the passing in and out of so many.
However, it is a recognised custom,
so much so that a smoking *foyer* is

101

attached to all the best theatres, and a warning bell is rung in it by the management a few minutes before the rising of the curtain.

Refreshments are frequently carried round by attendants to private boxes, and sometimes in the stalls

When refreshments are brought around. as well. Should they appear, it is the duty of the gentleman of the party to ask the lady or ladies if they wish for any, and to pay for what is consumed. It is, however, a rare thing for ladies to eat or drink at the play. The gentleman also pays for the programme at the few theatres where a charge is made.

I may mention, by the way, that it is not considered very good form to pay for programmes at theatres where the management makes no charge.

On unnecessary payment for programmes. Instances have been known where attendants have been discharged for accepting such fees ; and even apart from this, it is tantamount to presenting the attendant with sixpence or a shilling if one insists on paying for a programme or two provided free of charge. Many of the attendants are superior to accepting it.

AT A BALL.

THE etiquette of the ball-room is not
difficult to acquire, and yet there are
thousands of young men
going into society constantly
who flagrantly fail in it.
Their bad manners are con-
spicuous. They decline to dance unless
the prettiest girls in the room are
"trotted out" for them, block the door-
ways, haunt the refreshment-room, and
after supper promptly take their leave.
Could any course of conduct be in
worse taste? And what can a poor
hostess do? Young men are necessary
at dances, and they must be invited.
If they will not dance, who shall make
them? The delight of the
average hostess's heart is the
well-bred man, unspoiled by
conceit, who can always be
depended on to do his duty. He arrives
in good time, fills his card before very
long, and can be asked to dance with
a plain, neglected wallflower or two
without resenting it. He takes his
partner duly to the refreshment-room
after each dance, if she wishes to go,
and provides her with whatever she
wishes. Before leaving her, he sees her

*The eti-
quette of the
ball-room.*

*"The delight
of the
hostess's
heart."*

safe at her chaperon's side. If he should sit out a dance he returns in time to claim his partner for the next, not leaving her till it is half over, as is the wont of some young men. The truth

Self-denial the secret of good society.
is that society demands a never-ending series of self-denying actions from those who belong to it, and the more cheerfully these are performed, the more perfect are the manners. What can be more enjoyable than to sit in some cool retreat with a charming girl, enjoying one of those innocent flirtations that do so much to give zest to life ? But delightful though it be, the temptation to prolong it must be resisted, if an expectant partner is missing her dance and waiting in the ball-room to be claimed.

It is bad manners to go to a ball unless one is accomplished in the art of

Non-dancers should not accept invitations.
dancing. To do so is to take the place of one who may be more expert and therefore in greater request. Consequently, every man who wishes to be a success in society must learn to dance. There are abundant opportunities for doing so at the various dancing "academies," as they are rather unsuitably entitled, for there is not much about them of

The value of private lessons.
the academical, as generally understood. Private lessons are dearer than the others, but they are really necessary for most

men who have not been taught to
dance when boys. The whole attention of the teacher should be given
during the first three or four. A man
has so much to learn in addition to the
correct movements of his feet. He
must be taught to hold his head up,
to grasp his partner gently but firmly,
not to tread on her toes or knock his
knees against hers, and also how to
steer his course and hers in an imaginary
crowded room. Afterwards come the
finishing touches, when, per-

The finishing touches. fect in the steps and carriage
of the body, the learner is
taught to glide gently from foot to
foot, regulating his pace as quickly or
as slowly as he may wish. At first this
seems to be impossible, for the novice is
inclined to " rush his fences," as it were,
and he waltzes round the room at break-
neck speed, making himself giddy and
breathless, and sometimes causing dire
catastrophe. A girl finds it difficult to
forgive a man who has made her look
ridiculous. The fall of a couple is not
a frequent occurrence in a

A fall generally the man's fault. ball-room, but when it does
happen it is almost always
the man's fault. Girls take
much more naturally to the graceful
movements of the dance, and are,
besides, more often taught in childhood
than their brothers.

At a private ball the guest enters and
greets his hostess before speaking to
any one else. She shakes hands with

him and passes him on to some one
to introduce him to partners, perhaps

At a private
ball. her husband, perhaps her
son. With this beginning he
will probably get on very
well and may half-fill his card, and he
should take care to do so at once, for at
some balls the nice girls are immediately
snapped up and engaged for even the

The card
should be
filled early. extras before they have been
twenty minutes in the room.
"Are you engaged for every
dance, Miss Grey? Can you
spare me one?" And Miss Grey
probably gives him one, but if he is
a stranger of whose calisthenic prowess
nothing is known, she is careful to give
him only one. Sometimes his partners,
if they discover that he dances well,
introduce him to their sisters and
friends. If, however, he should find
himself left high and dry towards the
end of the evening, he should go back
to the gentlemen of the house and ask
them to introduce him to somebody else.
Young men of experience in such
matters usually manage very well
without this, but the novice has often
to face the alternative of dancing no
more or asking to be introduced. '

Hostesses sometimes make special
introductions for the "supper" dance,

The
"supper"
dance. the one immediately preceding that meal. This means
that the man introduced,
unless engaged to dance it
with some one else, is imperatively

called upon to accept the partner offered him and take her down to supper.

In asking a lady to dance it is usual to say, " Will you give me this waltz ? "
Asking a lady to dance. or " May I have this barn-dance ? " Some young men say, " Would you like to dance this ? Come along then ! " but such a form of address is only suited to intimates. When the dance is over, and the **After the dance.** partner left with her friends, the man says, " Thank you," bows, and leaves her.

If he wishes to see any lady to her carriage, he asks her per-**Seeing a lady to her carriage.** mission to do so, folds her wraps round her, hands her in, and stands until the carriage has gone some yards away.

ENGAGEMENT AND MARRIAGE.

THE old-fashioned rule that a man must approach the father of a girl before offering himself in marriage to her has now, to some extent, died out. At the same time it is considered dis-

A man may not propose when her family object. honourable for any one to propose to a girl in the face of the decided disapprobation of her family. Clandestine courtship is also regarded as dishonourable, except in circumstances where the girl is unhappy or oppressed and needs a champion. The usual way to ask for the admired one's hand in marriage is in

Proposal in person. person. This is always preferable to writing, though some men have not the courage to adopt the first course. Should the lady accept the offer, the happy wooer must take the earliest oppor-

Asking the father's permission. tunity of seeing her father, or, failing him, her nearest friend, and begging him to permit the engagement. Should he consent, all is well; but in the contrary case, his decision must be accepted. To allow a girl to engage herself against the wish of her family is to drag her into a false position. Very often submission to the decree effects more towards procuring its reversal than violent opposition. It is difficult, of course, for young people to be patient, but if they can only manage a little of it they would find the truth of the French proverb, "All things come round to those who know how to wait."

Should the father refuse consent.

Immediately upon having the engagement ratified, the accepted suitor gives the lady an engagement ring. This should be as handsome a present as he can afford to buy. Together with all other presents and correspondence on both sides, this ring must be returned if the engagement should be broken off.

The engagement ring.

The accepted man is in duty bound to spend most of his leisure with his intended bride. He must not go off for a sojourn abroad while she is spending some weeks by the sea in England, unless she has expressed a wish to that effect. It would be a considerable "snub" to her to do so. Society has sometimes been amused by the announcement one day of a "marriage having been arranged between Mr. A. and Miss B.," and on the next of the intention of Mr. A. to start for a tour round the world. This almost

One's duty to one's betrothed.

A significant announcement.

always means that the man has been entrapped into a proposal, and would willingly retreat if he honourably could. Such things happen only too often. Manœuvring mothers have much to answer for in the matter. Worldly girls have often sufficient wisdom of the serpent to bring a reluctant wooer to the point and, by immediately announcing the engagement to their friends, to make it extremely difficult for him to retreat.

Sometimes a girl falls so wildly in love with a man that she creates a kind of corresponding, though passing, fervour in him, and while it lasts he believes himself in love, though his emotions are only a mixture of gratified **When a girl takes the initiative.** vanity and that physical attraction which needs true love to redeem it from the fleshly sort. Should marriage follow upon such courtships as these, where the girl takes ever the initiative, the union is very seldom a happy one. The wife never feels sure that her husband really loves her or would have chosen her. She knows that he was her choice, rather than she his, and a racking jealousy seizes her and makes her not only miserable herself, but a very uncomfortable companion for him. He, too, often finds when it is too late that she fulfils none **The unhappy sequel.** of his ideals, and is in many ways a contrast to the girl he would have chosen if she had not whirled him into the vortex of her own strong feeling. And he occasionally wonders if she may not some day experience a similar strength of attraction for some other man and let herself be carried away by it as she had been by her feeling for him. "Hot fires soon burn out," he thinks, and remembers the warning given to Othello: "She hath deceived her father, and may thee." No man should

Long engagements. drag a girl into a long engagement. Nor should any man propose to a girl until he is in a position to provide for her. He is only standing in the way of other wooers who may be well supplied with this world's gear. Such

And unsuitable positions. trifles as wealth and ease may appear as nought to the mind of the youthful lover, not to be weighed for a moment in the balance with love and young romance. The girl, too, may be of the same way of thinking at the time, but it the more behoves the man, the stronger, to consider her and to remember

A man's duty to look at cold facts. that poverty is such a bitter and a cruel thing that it even kills love at times. Recrimination in the home is a hard thing to bear. And yet how many millions of women since the world began have said to their husband: "Oh, why did I ever marry you? I could have done so much better."

And how many men have said to

their wives : " Well ! You were determined to have me, so now you must
make the best of me."

However, we will suppose these rocks
and quicksands past, the engaged couple
happy, and the wedding day at hand.

Custom demands that the
The bridegroom's obligations. bridegroom shall present her
bouquet to the bride, as well
as bouquets and a present
each to the bridesmaids. He must
furnish the house for the bride in every
detail, not excepting the house and
table linen, which, in the old days of
spinning-wheels, was wont to be con-
tributed by the bride herself.

He must provide the wedding ring
and the carriage in which his best man
and himself go to church. He pays
the fees to clergyman and
The best man. clerk, but it is the best man
who hands them over. With
him the bridegroom waits at the altar
till the bride arrives. She takes her
place at his left hand for the first time,
and at the proper moment he produces
the ring which is the symbol of their
union.

The usual dress of a bridegroom consists of a very dark blue
The bridegroom's dress. frock-coat, light trousers,
light or white scarf-tie,
patent boots, and a new hat.

DRESS.

It is absolutely true, though in a very
limited sense, that the tailor makes the
man. If a man does not
dress well in society he cannot be a success. If he
commits flagrant errors in costume he
will not be invited out very much, of
that he may be certain. If he goes to
a garden party in a frock-coat and
straw hat, he is condemned
more universally than if
he had committed some
crime. The evidence of the
latter would not be upon him for all
men to read, as the evidence of his
ignorance in social forms is, in his mis-
taken notions of dress. Things are
more involved than ever in the sartorial
line, since so many new sports and
pastimes have sprung up for men. A
man cannot consult his tailor upon
every trifling detail, even if his tailor
were always a perfectly re-
liable authority, which is not
always the case, for there
are tailors and tailors. A
young man's finances do not always
allow him to go to one of the best, and
the second and third-rate artists in

Importance of dress.

The penalty of solocisms of costume.

Tailors not always to be relied on.

B3

cloth are apt to purvey second and third-rate fashions to their customers.

A brief summary of the forms of dress appropriate to various occasions may be of some use to the inexperienced. It is obvious that to enter into detail would be out of place in a matter where change is the order of the day. But there are

"Certain fixed rules." certain fixed rules that are, in a sense, permanent, and with these I may succinctly deal.

For morning wear the morning-coat or jacket or the tweed suit is correct.

For morning wear. After lunch, when in town, the well-dressed man may continue to wear his morning-coat or the regulation frock-coat, with trousers of some neat, striped grey mixture. The tailor's name for the material of these is " mixed cheviots."

Light trousers. It is not considered good form to wear very light trousers except on special occasions, such as weddings, garden parties, or afternoon assemblies of a festive kind. Even then it is better to err on the quiet side than to be overloud. The days of broadcloth have long gone by, and coats are now made

Black coats. of vicuna cloth or black twilled worsteds, with a dull finish and of an elastic quality. Waistcoats may be single or double-breasted. There is no restriction as to the colour of the tie.

The Park suit may consist of a grey

or light-brown frock-coat, with waistcoat and trousers to match,
The Park suit. and this is the usual dress
for Ascot, the smartest of all
the races. At Sandown the low hat
and tweed suit, or long racing coat, are
worn, except on such days as the Princess of Wales is present, when the
Prince sets the example of wearing a
black coat and silk hat, and all other
men are expected to follow his example.

For a morning walk in the Park in
summer the straw hat, or low hat and
tweed suit, are as correct as
For a summer morning in the Park. the black coat and silk hat.
But it must be remembered
that a straw hat or low hat
cannot be worn with a black coat of
any kind. The "pot" hat and brown
boots are permissible with an overcoat,
Brown boots. under which there may be a
tweed suit, but brown boots
may not otherwise accompany a black
coat, though they are admissible with
the Ascot suit.

There are special suits for all kinds
of outdoor amusements, such as shoot-
Special suits. ing, golfing, tennis, boating,
driving, riding, bicycling,
fishing, hunting, &c., but into the details of these it is unnecessary to enter.
It may be remarked, how-
Spoiling an otherwise good effect. ever, that it is easy to stultify
the whole effect of these,
however perfectly they may
be "built" by the tailor, by the acci-

115

tion of a single incongruous article of attire ; such as a silk hat or patent boots with a shooting-suit.

The dress-coat is no longer made of broadcloth, the shiny finish of which would now have a very old-fashioned appearance. The ordinary evening coat is made of an elastic twill cloth, with a dull finish. Its elasticity makes it fit to perfection when cut by a good tailor. Of course it would be incorrect to wear other than black trousers with it. The waistcoat is much cut away, to show a wide expanse of immaculately got-up shirt-front.

The modern dress-coat.

This is the only correct costume for evening wear on all occasions of a formal nature. The dinner-jacket has very largely superseded the dress-coat for home wear and at dinners in houses where one is a familiar guest. It is occasionally seen at the play, too, but it would be incorrect to wear it when accompanying ladies.

The dinner-jacket.

Etiquette is not now nearly so strict as it used to be in the matter of evening dress in the stalls, private boxes, and dress circle of the theatres. I think this is rather to be deplored, but the wave of democracy that has poured over society of late has left its impress in this as in other matters. Though theatre managers put on the tickets special to the best seats " Even-

On evening dress at theatres.

DRESS.

ing Dress," I have seen half-a-dozen men in the stalls dressed in a variety of unorthodox fashions, and once, in August, I even saw a man in a boating suit come in, straw hat in hand, and, ushered by an unprotesting attendant, take his seat. In the off-season, when all the fashionable people are out of town, this was not, perhaps, very surprising. But he must have been a courageous young man.

A courageous young man.

Mourning for men seems almost a dead-letter nowadays, except in the first two or three weeks after bereavement. A widower's mourning is not worn for more than a couple of months, unless the widower should belong to the numerous class who cling conservatively to old customs, and believe that to doff his weeds would imply some disrespect to his late wife.

Mourning dress.

Disraeli, in his "Endymion," puts the following words in the mouth of Mr. Vigo, the great tailor :—

"Dress does not make a man, but it often makes a successful one. The most precious stone, you know, must be cut and polished. I have known many an heiress lost by her suitor being ill-dressed. You must dress according to your age, your pursuits, your object in life; you must dress, too, in some cases, according to your set. In youth a little fancy is

"Dress does not make a man."

117

rather expected, but if political life be
your object, it should be avoided—at
least after one-and-twenty. I am

"But it often
makes a
successful
one."

dressing two brothers now,
men of considerable posi-
tion; one is a mere man
of pleasure, the other will
probably be a Minister of State. They
are as like as two peas, but were I to
dress the dandy and the minister the
same, it would be bad taste—it would
be ridiculous. No man gives me the
trouble which Lord Eglantine does;
he has not made up his mind whether
he will be a great poet or a Prime
Minister. 'You must choose, my lord,'
I tell him. 'I cannot send you out
looking like Lord Byron if you mean
to be a Canning or a Pitt.'

"What all men should avoid is the
'shabby genteel.' No man ever gets
over it. I will save you from that.
You had better be in rags."

COUNTRY LIFE.

DRESS in the country varies considerably in many matters from that worn in town. A boy's first

Dress in the country. "country suit" after he leaves school is a great event to him. At Eton and Harrow the style of dress might almost be called a uniform, and the first suit of tweeds marks the emanci-

The first suit of tweeds. pation from school-life. When in the country he dons these the first thing in the morning, unless he should be on hunting or bicycling thoughts intent, or should incline towards tennis, boating, or the slow delights of angling. After lunch a change has occasionally to be made.

Should a garden party be in question, he may take his choice between tweed suit and low hat or

At a garden party. cutaway coat with silk hat. If he happen to be great on tennis the tweed suit would be naturally his choice, unless it were distinctly understood that the game would form a prominent feature of the afternoon's entertainment. In this case flannels would be worn. Sometimes very ceremonious garden parties take place in the country, when Royalty or distinguished persons are expected to be present, when the frock coat and its usual accompaniments would not be out of place.

Invitations to breakfast in the country are by no means unusual. The dress would consist of that ordinarily worn in the mornings, whether tweed suit, knickerbockers, hunting or riding gear, or the black morning-coat or suit. Frequently a silk hat is never seen between Sunday and Sunday. Churchgoers still, to a certain extent, affect it, but in these days of outdoor life, bicycling, and so on, the costume worn by men in church is experiencing the same modifications that characterise it in other departments. The details of shooting suits can always be studied in the illustrated advertisements of the tailors. A man's wardrobe is now almost as varied as a woman's. He has different costumes for walking, riding, driving, visiting, boating, hunting, shooting, golfing, bicycling, tennis, and cricket, dining, smoking, and lounging, football, racing, and yachting, to say nothing of uniform and Court suit, besides the now developing motor-car costume.

Invitations to breakfast.

Church-going costume.

VISITING-CARDS AND CALLS.

It is necessary for every young man to have a supply of visiting-cards, and for

Visiting-cards, size and style.

these there is one fixed rule, any departure from which betokens want of knowledge of the customs of well-bred people. The size must be exactly three inches by one and a half. The pasteboard must be pure white and glossy and the lettering must be in italic.

An idea prevails among young men of a certain class that it is incorrect to

The customary or other title must precede the name.

put the title "Mr." before their own name on a visiting-card. This is a great mistake. Not to put it is to show oneself lacking in *savoir faire*. The name must always be preceded by "Mr." or "Sir," or other title. The address must occupy the left-hand corner, and the name of one's club or clubs must follow it.

In the absence of a permanent address.

When a young man has no permanent address, it is well to have only his name printed, filling in the address in pencil before leaving or presenting his card.

The hours for calling are from four to seven in the afternoon, but young men who are not on very intimate terms with the family should carefully abstain from calling after six o'clock, lest they should be the last and solitary caller.

The hours for calling.

When the door is opened, and the question, "Is Mrs. Blank at home?" answered in the affirmative, the visitor is invited to follow the servant. He may take off his overcoat if he wishes, but he must carry his hat and stick in his hand. The right-hand glove must be removed. The gloved hand is never given to a lady, certain exceptional circumstances proving the rule. Arrived in the drawing-room, he holds his hat and glove in the left hand, greets his hostess first, she shaking hands with him, and then he looks round the room and greets any acquaintance he may recognise, going up to them if he knows them well, bowing if his previous knowledge of them has been slight. Having taken his seat, he still holds his hat in his hand, and he must find small talk as best he can, for sitting silent is awkward for him and distressing to his hostess. She, by the way, will probably say, "Would you not like to put down your hat?" indicating some spot where he may lay it. The reason of carrying the hat to the drawing-room

On arrival.

Greeting the hostess.

is a somewhat subtle one. It is based on the supposition that the masculine caller feels himself privileged

The reason why the hat is carried. in being permitted to pay his respects, and feeling himself on sufferance, is ready to leave in a moment, hat in hand, should he not find his presence agreeable and acceptable.

I have a private theory that this custom is cherished and kept up by men from a conviction that their hats are much safer in their own sight in the drawing-room than they would be downstairs in the hall. New umbrellas have been taken instead of old, as we all know, and new hats are quite as tempting, if not more so.

Do not send your card up when making a call. This is reserved for business men. The servant

The card should not be sent up. asks your name, and it must be given very distinctly. It will then be announced in a loud, clear voice when the door is opened. Should the hostess show by her manner that she has not recognised the name, its owner must recall himself to her memory by saying, " I am Mr. So-and-so. I had the pleasure of," &c., &c., explaining the circumstances that led to the call.

Leaving the card on departure. The visiting-card must be left on the hall table when the caller goes away, one card for the ladies of the house, and one for the gentleman or gentlemen, whether these latter have been present or absent during the call.

Should the lady called on be " Not at home" the cards are given to the servant.

When a man has rendered an unknown lady some really important service, as in the case of a **Rendering an important service.** street accident or some other disagreeable circumstance in which he has been able to avert from her some unpleasantness which she would have otherwise incurred, the lady will probably ask him to let her know to whom she is indebted for so much kindness. The proper course to pursue is to disclaim any special obligation, but if the lady persists, it is then good manners to give the name. Should the gentleman feel very much interested in the lady, he may say, " I should very much like to call to-morrow to find out if you are none the worse for your adventure." She may then give him her address, and he would give her his card.

But this would all be very much out of place if the affair had been some mere matter of common **A trivial service.** courtesy, such as picking up some article dropped by a lady and restoring it to her. A gentleman in such circumstances raises his hat and retires as quickly as possible, lest the lady should imagine that he could base a claim to her acquaintance on the performance of so trivial a service.

It is only the "cad" who thus presumes, and the "cad-ess" who allows him to do so.

Visiting-cards are never sent by post. They denote a call in person. The only exception to this rule **P. P. C. Cards.** is in sending out P. P. C. cards. These are always sent by post. The letters denote *pour prendre congé* ("to take leave"), and are used when it is found impossible to call and say goodbye to all one's circle of acquaintance.

A call after a ball or dinner-party must be made within the week, and cards left. In calling to inquire after the welfare of an invalid, or after the family has suffered bereave- **Sickness and death.** ment, cards are always left. If a man is on intimate terms with a family that has suffered bereavement, he sometimes uses cards with a slight line of black, and should he write a letter of condolence, note-paper and envelopes with the same slight indication of mourning on them. This expresses sympathy and a personal share in the sorrow felt.

In making a call after death has visited any family, the dress of the caller should be attuned to the occasion, and should be of a sombre order, though it need not be precisely mourning.

When a man is a frequent visitor to

any house, he may leave his hat and stick in the hall.

The umbrella is never taken into a drawing-room.

After an invitation. Cards must be left after an invitation, whether the latter be accepted or not.

In case of not wishing to pursue the acquaintance of the person who sent the invitation, it is sufficient to leave the cards without inquiring whether the lady is at home.

If a man should wish, for any reason, to courteously end an acquaintanceship, **Terminating an acquaintanceship with courtesy.** he can do it without any of the intolerable "cutting," a method resorted to only by the rough and uncultivated.

He may make a call that, in his own mind, he knows to be a final one, remaining only just the quarter of an **The final call.** hour that is the minimum length of such functions, and preserving a certain gravity of demeanour which is as free from "sulks" as it is from other forms of bad temper. After this, he may leave cards once more without asking if the ladies of the family are at home. In this way he can gradually and with perfect courtesy break off the intimacy.

In the street. In the street he raises his hat but does not stop to speak. It is quite possible to ignore the attempt to do so on the opposite side, but should circumstances be such as to make it difficult to do so without positive rudeness, he must stop, putting an end to the conversation at the earliest possible moment.

A call should never extend over half an hour unless the caller be expressly requested to prolong it. A gentleman never looks at his watch during a call, at a dinner-party, afternoon reception or ball. This is prohibited because the inference would be that time was dragging with him and that he was anxious to get away. A man may feel such anxiety, but he must hide it if he would be deemed well-bred.

Duration of call.

Consulting the watch.

Young men who do not pay their duty call and leave a card after any entertainment, are likely to be omitted from the list of guests invited on some succeeding occasion.

Occasionally it happens that a young man finds himself " dropped " by some family with whom he has been on terms of intimacy. He is debarred by the rules of polite society from asking for an explanation, it being a canon of good breeding never to ask questions that are embarrassing to reply to. This has been embodied in a very outspoken and unceremonious phrase "you ask me no questions, I tell you no lies." There is a deep truth in it, nevertheless, and even in family life it is well to observe it.

When a man finds himself " dropped."

Sometimes the reason a young man

is dropped in this way is that something to his disadvantage has been dis-
covered. But not unfrequently the true
reason is that one of the daughters of
the house has shown a
An occasional reason. preference for his society
which the parents think
should be checked. Girls of the
present day do not always exercise the
well-bred self-control that is the rule of
good society in such matters. To love
unsought is a misfortune for any girl,
leading inevitably to much mortification
and humiliation, but these may be
minimised if she can only practice a
dignified reticence about her feelings.

But should a young man thus
capriciously (as it seems to him) be
left out in the cold be on
Putting out a feeler. sufficiently good terms with
a son of the house, it would
be quite in rule for him to put out a
feeler or two on the subject : " I say,
old fellow, I wonder if I have been so
unfortunate as to offend your people in
any way ? " He will soon discover,
from the aspect of his interlocutor,
whether he is likely to gain any information on the matter.

CALLS OF INQUIRY.

In calling on friends who have suffered
bereavement, after having received their
card of thanks for kind inquiries, it is,
of course, requisite that the dress should

be of the quietest description. A red
tie, for instance, would be horribly out
of place. Only in case of
Calling on friends bereaved. very intimate friendships is
the call prolonged beyond
ten minutes or a quarter
of an hour. The caller takes his
tone from that of the family. It is
in the worst taste to refer to the
loss sustained unless the initiative is
taken by one of those
Avoiding reference to the loss. bereaved. This is very
seldom done, and the
conversation is usually con-
ducted on lines calculated to avert any
disturbing remark. No one likes to
break down or lose self-command
except in seclusion; and, in fact, it
is only necessary to look into one's
own consciousness in order to discover what is the best course to
follow in such cases.

Should a young man be invited to
attend the funeral, he must wear
mourning, black gloves, and
Attending the funeral. black hatband. Punctuality,
important at all times, is
particularly essential at this dreary
ceremonial. The family usually provides carriages, but in the case of
friends who possess equipages, they
always take their own. It is the
custom to assemble at the house, or
to go by fixed train should
Invitations to return. the family reside in the
country. It is better not
to accept any invitations to return to

the house afterwards ; for, as a rule, these are only given as a matter of form.

We often see in newspapers after the announcement of a death, a request that no flowers may be sent. Failure to comply with this would argue a want of perception, but when no such intimation is made a friend may send flowers, the only essential being that they should consist as a rule of pure white flowers or orchids, pansies, or violets. Occasionally an exception is made to these in the case of favourite flowers of the lost friend. An exquisite garland of pale tea-roses appeared among the scores of wreaths seen at the funeral of one of our greatest poets.

Gifts of flowers:

MANNER.

It would not be easy to over-estimate
the importance of a good manner from
a social point of view. It
ranks far above much more
important qualities. The
"rough diamonds" who
conceal their traditional good heart
under a surly exterior are seldom
happy people, notwithstanding their
genuine thoroughness and real goodness. In family life and in society a
gentle manner "covers a multitude of
sins." The world and the home reflect
back to us the face we present to them.
If we cultivate a bright and cordial
manner we shall be heartily received
by others, though the real nature of
us lies beneath as cold and
hard as salt fresh from a
mine. In the home the
coldness and hardness are
soon found out, but they are partially
condoned for the sake of the superficial courtesy and kindness. In society
the quality of the heart matters little,
so long as the surface is, at
the same time, genial and
polished. Life is chiefly
made up of small things,
and if we learn to take an interest in

*The
importance
of a good
manner.*

*The qualities
valued by
society.*

*"Life is a
large bundle
of little
things."*

the trifling incidents of our friends' lives, in the everyday occurrences in the existence of our acquaintances, we supply the sympathetic element that tells so largely in our favour. And very often the simulation of this interest induces the reality, and our own life is brightened by participating in the pleasures and the happiness of others, and deepened by sharing in their disappointments, and by doing so helping them to overcome them. With a cold, forbidding manner it is impossible to convey any such impression. But this often comes from shyness, not only in the young, but all through life. The youthful form of shyness is self-consciousness and self-distrust. That which lasts through life is the fear of self-revelation. Even the frankest natures have often this quality of reticence, which forbids them to reveal the inner depths of their thoughts, and makes them hate to be divined.

Simulation may induce reality.

Shyness.

And reticence.

Rochefoucauld says we all hate to be divined, though we like to divine others ; but many of us know well what a delightful thing it is to be read like an open book by those whose thoughts reflect our own, and with whom we discover ourselves to be in mental kinship.

The ideal life is that which has few friends but many acquaintances. The

friends are close and firm ones, "grap-
pled to our hearts with hooks of steel,"

The ideal life—few friends, many ac-quaintances. and the circle of acquaintances offers opportunities for
adding to their number. But
without an agreeable manner
it is difficult to secure these
inner and outer spheres of social companionship. Were I asked to give

A recipe for the formation of a good manner. a recipe for the formation
of a good manner I should
recommend an equal mix-
ture of self-confidence and
humility as the first essential, then a
considerable desire to please, tempered
by the self-respect which preserves
from officiousness and that annoying
air of "ingratiating" themselves that
some men assume in society. There
must be perfect self-possession, though
in the very young this is scarcely
expected, a little becoming shyness
sitting very well upon them. "I like a
shy man. He's getting so scarce," said
a very pretty woman at a ball not long
since. "Find one, quick, and introduce
him." Her laughing emissaries went
off to search for the desired article,
and after a while returned with the
report that the only shy man in the
room was engaged for every dance !

Add gentle-ness to self-possession. When self-possession has been acquired it is well to add on
to it the saving grace of
gentleness. This quality is
much misunderstood by
men. In women they adore it ; in

themselves and each other they under-value it. But women love gentleness in men. It is a most telling piece of the necessary equipment for society. A gentle manner, a gentle voice, and the absence of all self-assertion, that is at the root of the matter, have won more love than good looks.

Carlyle called the members of upper-class society " amiable stoics," in refer-ence to the equable serenity of countenance and calm self-possession of manner with which they accept those occa-sionally trying conditions of social life which necessitate self-denial in matters great and small. This placidity is the result of long training. Not just at first does a young man bow to the decree of his hostess which separates him from the girl he admires and tells him off to take some uninteresting dowager to the supper-room. But should he evince any sign of discon-tent with the arrangement he is at once convicted of ill-breeding. The man of "perfect manners" is he who is calmly cour-teous in all circumstances, as attentive outwardly to the plain and the elderly as he is to the young and pretty. It is difficult to renounce the delightful *tête-à-tête* with a charming girl when asked by his hostess to dance with some poor wall-flower who has been neglected for half-a-dozen dances. But it has to

"Amiable stoics."

The man of "perfect manners."

be borne, and eventually it brings its own reward. The "duty" dance is a hard thing, and good manners involve a considerable amount of self-denial ; but repetition soon makes it comparatively easy, and invitations of an agreeable kind pour in on the young man who shows himself willing to practise those peculiar forms of self-lessness, opportunities for which so frequently arise in society.

Self-denial not unrewarded.

It is probably in imitation of this surface equanimity that the wooden stare has been adopted so universally by our golden youth. This is useful for wearing at one's club or in the stall of a theatre, and it at once stamps the proprietor of the stare as being " in it." The fashion is not confined to England. It reigns in New York, and even in far Australia there is a select coterie of golden or gilded youth who are beginning to learn how to abstract every atom of expression from the countenance, and to lock on vacancy or seem to do so. As yet, there is no considerable expertness achieved in the matter in Antipodean circles, but in New York a very fair impression of imbecility is conveyed in the look of the ultra-fashionable young man. There are various other important matters on which a transatlantic authority has been instructing the youth of his generation. The one

The wooden stare.

involving the most serious responsi-
bility is connected with carrying a cane
or stick, as it is better form to call it.
It must be left at home when going to
business, to church, or to make calls.
The idea of the latter prohibition is
that, if a call is made on a lady cane
in hand, the inference would be that
the caller is on sufficiently intimate
terms to look in on her casually at
any time. There is certainly

Transatlantic
etiquette.
subtlety in this view. It is
well that the novice should
be made aware that the lowest depth
of vulgarity is touched by carrying an
umbrella in a case. It is also an important item of information that the
gloves and cane must be carried in
the same hand. To do otherwise is
seriously to err in social forms. Our
instructor declares that to attend
oratorios and philharmonic concerts
is thoroughly bad form, indicating a
tendency to be pedantic. It is much
better to go to a horse show. It is by
no means considered correct to shake
hands. The proper way is to take hold
of the fingers of one's acquaintance at
the second joints, and bestow upon
them one or two decisive little jerks,
as though testing their strength. "No,
I thank you," is a form of words no
longer heard in good society, having
some time since been replaced by "No,
thanks." No man with any claim to
social position would consent to pronounce the "g" at the end of the

present participle of verbs. " Comin'
and goin' " are the correct forms just
now. " Don't you know " is ridicu-
lously correct. Men of perception do
not care to be more accurate than
others of their set. " Don't-chi-know "
is more customary, and the pronuncia-
ton marks the man as riding on the
topmost crest of the social wave.
There must be a staccato sound about
the phrase, which alternates pleasantly
with the languid drawl. The latter is
still in favour, and accompanies admir-
ably the studied lack of animation in
the expression and general wooden
look of the face.

To revert for a moment to the cane,
or. walking-stick. There is much to be
deduced from the manner in which it

The stick. is carried. The correct style
is to hold it at an angle of
forty-five degrees, with the ferule upper-
most and forward. This is the sort of
thing that no man could possibly discover for himself. The natural man
would incline to carry his stick in such
fashion as would tend to direct its point
to the ground. This unsophisticated
mode would at once reveal him as
uninitiated in the minor morals of good

The hair. manners. The latest mode
of arranging the male hair,
as practised in New York, and possibly
nearer home as well, is worth noting.
First it is made thoroughly wet, then
brushed and parted, after which the
head is swathed with linen bands,

which are kept on until the hair is thoroughly dry. This method produces the plastered appearance which is now recognised as good form. Though cordiality of manner is rapidly becoming obsolete, and is utterly condemned by all who have studied the subject, yet it is a recognised fact

Amiability.

that amiability has now superseded sarcasm, and the up-to-date young man practises a careless superficial benevolence of pronouncing every woman charming and every man a good fellow. The scathing, satiric wit of the last century was as the nadir to this zenith of appreciative recognition of the best that is in every human being.

It is pleasant to be able to add to all this minute detail about little superficialities that the young man of to-day is a vast improvement on his predecessors in very many ways. Swearing is out of fashion. Getting intoxicated is decidedly "low," and those who disgrace themselves in this way are soon cut by their acquaint-

The rowdyism of twenty years ago.

ance. Some twenty years since things were very different. To get tipsy was regarded as a proof of manliness. To wrench off door-knockers and play similar senseless pranks was considered a form of wit, and the heroes of such performances were looked on with admiring eyes by their companions.

In many ways a higher standard now

reigns. The pictures of ballet dancers
that used once to adorn a
A higher moral standard now reigns. young man's rooms have
given place to others of a
higher class. Dissolute and
unprincipled men get the cold shoulder
from others of their set, and vice, thank
Heaven, is thoroughly out of fashion.
There is still plenty of folly. It is
inseparable from youth. But in matters
of more moment there has been im-
mense improvement going steadily on
for many years.

There are young men who mistake
arrogance of manners for self-possession, and who conduct
Arrogance of manners. themselves, when in society
with lifted chin and a
haughty air that may accord very well
with their own estimate of themselves,
but seem rather out of place to on-
lookers. Such a man invites com-
parisons between his social deserts and
his implied conviction of superiority.
He may take in a few inexperienced
girls and young fellows of adolescent
inability of judgment, but even these
triumphs are short-lived, and he is set
down as a " pompous ass," to use the
young man's phrase for describing him.

It is good manners to articulate
distinctly, and bad manners to neglect
to do so. A man need not
Distinct articulation. exactly take lessons in elo-
cution (though they would
not be amiss), but he can teach himself to pronounce clearly and use the

tone of voice that is best suited to
the various occasions when
Tones of voice. he converses. A breathy
voice is extremely disagree-
able. The syllables come out enveloped
in a sort of windy roar. This is owing
to a wrong way of breathing, and it
can easily be cured, with advantage to
the health as well as the personality.
A very confidential tone is always used
by some men when they speak to
women. If they merely
The confi- dential tone. "hope your gown did not
get muddy" they look into
one's eyes and murmur like any suck-
ing dove. But if their articulation is
indistinct they are quite a nuisance.
One has to ask them to repeat themselves, and the nonsense they talk
shows up very badly in an *encore*.
But when they enunciate clearly their
devoted murmurings sometimes "take"
very well. It is not until a woman has
seen three or four others besides herself approached in the same afternoon
or evening with similar devout and
prayer-like whispering that she begins to
value this particularity at its true worth.

With reference to the word "fellow"
a subtle distinction or two must be
drawn. In lowly circles a
The word "fellow." young man is called "a
fellow"; young men "fel-
lows." So it is in good society, but
with a distinct difference. It is not
very easy to make this difference clear.
Young men of good position refer very

commonly to others of their acquaintance as "the fellows," but they would
not use the word to describe young
men generally. Women, young and
old, of the lower classes speak of
young men generally as "fellows," but
gentlewomen never do so. A lady
never uses the expression "A girl and
a fellow." At the same time she may
frequently speak of "young fellows."
I am aware that there is a want of
clearness in all this, but it is a matter
among many others that can only be
acquired by being accustomed to the
usages of good society.

The Autocrat of the Breakfast-table
said in one of his books that if he
heard a woman pronounce
the word "How," he learned
more about her in an instant
than a third person could
tell him in an hour. If she called
it "haow," she revealed herself as
belonging to the uncultured classes.
In the same way, if a girl were to say
"I met a fellow yesterday," she would
unconsciously make a similar
self-revelation. A young
man would make an equal
mistake if he were to speak
of "my sister's fellow." But he would
be correct enough if he were to say
"the fellow my sister's engaged to."

These little *nuances* of expression
remind one of the old rhyme—

"Strange that such difference should be
'Twixt tweedledum and tweedledee."

141

Though small talk is as indispensable in social life as pennies and half pennies in the transactions of everyday existence, we must also have conversational gold and silver at our command if we wish to be successful. When the preliminaries of acquaintanceship are over there is no necessity to keep up the commonplaces of small talk. To do so is rather insulting to women. To be "talked down to" is always aggravating, especially when one feels a conviction that the person who is thus affably stooping for one's benefit belongs in reality to a lower intellectual plane than one's own. At the same time, many young men "with nothing in them" are socially successful, being possessed of those superficial qualities and that outward polish which are, for the purposes of everyday intercourse, more useful than abysmal personal depths. Was it Goethe or Schiller who said that for domestic utility a farthing candle is more useful than all the stars of heaven?

Small talk alone will not suffice.

"Talking down" really an insult.

Yet polish alone often succeeds.

A light playfulness of fancy, combined with the gentleness that carefully avoids wounding even the smallest, is a high recommendation in society; but to be for ever laughing is wearisome in the extreme to the spectators.

I make no apology for quoting here

the following passages from "Mr.
Brown's Letters to a Young
Man About Town" from a
Punch of 1849. "Mr. Brown"
was Thackeray, I believe.

"Mr. Brown's" advice.

He says :—

"I beseech and implore you to
make a point of being intimate with
one or two families where you can
see kind and well-bred English ladies.
I have seen women of all nations in
the world, but I never saw the equals
of English women (meaning, of course,
to include our cousins the MacWhirters
of Glasgow and the O'Tooles of Cork) ;
and I pray sincerely, my boy, that
you may always have a woman for a
friend."

*   *   *   *

"It is better for you to pass an evening once or twice a week in a lady's
drawing-room, even though the conversation is rather slow and you know
the girl's songs by heart, than in a club,
tavern, or smoking-room, or pit of a
theatre."

*   *   *   *

"Remember, if a house is pleasant,
and you like to remain in it, that to be
well with the women of the house is the
great, the vital point. If it is a good
house, don't turn up your nose because
you are only asked to come in the evening, while others are invited to dine.
Recollect the debts of dinners which

an hospitable family has to pay ; who
are you that you should always be
expecting to nestle under the maho-
gany ? Agreeable acquaintances are
made just as well in the drawing-
room as in the dining-room. Go to
tea brisk and good-humoured. Be
determined to be pleased. Talk to a
dowager. Take a hand at whist. If
you are musical, and know a song,
sing it like a man. Never sulk about
dancing, but off with you. You
will find your acquaintance enlarge.
Mothers, pleased with your good
humour, will probably ask you to
Pocklington Square, to a little party.
You will get on—you will form yourself
a circle. You may marry a rich girl,
or, at any rate, get the chance of
seeing a number of the kind and the
pretty."

*   *   *   *

" The dressing, the clean gloves, and
cab-hire, are nuisances, I grant you.
The idea of the party itself is a bore,
but you must go. When you are at
the party, it is not so stupid ; there is
always something pleasant for the eye
and attention of an observant man."

IN CHURCH.

I KNOW a young man who makes it
a practice to arrive late in church
every Sunday. I often wish

On arriving late at church. that he did not go to ny
church, for he makes me
cordially despise him, thus
disturbing the calm and quiet of the
proper frame of mind for Sundays. I
conclude that he likes to be looked at,
though why he should do so is not
apparent. It is, in fact, not only rude,
but irreverent, to be late in church for
the beginning of the service. If one
should be accidentally late, it is good
manners to wait till the congregation
rises from the kneeling posture before
making one's way to a seat. It is
almost an awful thing to interrupt a
prayer. But I have seen people do it
with no more scruple than if they were
passing in a crowded street.

Eighteen inches are the measure-
ment of space allowed to each sitter
in the churches. In some

On the space one may occupy. it may be more ; in others
it may be less. But I
have reason to believe that
this is the average. Now, if any man
of extra size should find himself in a
pew with other persons, he must, in

11   145

common courtesy, keep himself as
well within the limits of eighteen
inches as the width of his shoulders
will allow. But I have occasionally
seen quite slim young men sprawl far
beyond the frontier lines. Lounging

Lounging. · is a habit of the day, and
there are men who get themselves into marvellously corkscrew
attitudes, in church as elsewhere.
Fidgety men are more so in church

Fidgety
men.
than anywhere else. They
seem to find it impossible to
keep still. Sometimes they
even produce a cough wherewith to
amuse themselves, though they are
not troubled with it at any other time.
The charm of a reposeful manner is
denied to them. Reverence for the
sacred place conduces to a quiet
manner ; but this is not always felt
by those who attend public worship.

The conven-
tional idea
of church
attendance.
The conventional idea seems
to be that such assemblies
are merely phases of social
life ; that it is respectable to
be seen there ; and that the service
and the sermon are things to be
worried through in deference to a
prevalent idea that they form part
of an institution that is generally
regarded as excellent. The small

The true
light to re-
gard the
services in.
minority are those who regard church services in their
true light as lifting the
thoughts above earthly
things, and yet by no means unfitting

146

them for earth. Where, for instance, could a better law of good manners be found than in the Book of Books? A glance at the end of the fourth chapter of Ephesians will show a code of conduct that, if followed, would make a man a perfect member of society.

CORRESPONDENCE.

IT is impolite to leave letters un-answered for several days, especially if the writers are ladies, or, if **Replying to letters.** men, superior in age or station. Notes of invitation should be replied to within twenty-four hours. Plain white cream-laid note-paper and envelopes should be used, the latter either square or **Writing materials.** wallet-shaped, but never of the oblong, narrow shape peculiar to business correspondence. The address on the notepaper should be embossed or printed in simple characters, over-ornament being in the worst taste. If the writer is entitled to use a crest, it should be produced as simply as possible, with or without the family motto, and free from the glow of varied colour in which some men and women delight. There are letters whose devices in scarlet and gold are strangely in contrast with the meagre and disappointing character of their contents. They make one think of fried sprats served up on a gold entrée dish.

The writing should be clear, neat

and legible, the ink black. In beginning a letter with "Sir" or "Madam," the omission of the name is remedied by inscribing it in the left-hand corner at the bottom of the note. In commercial correspondence it seems to be the rule to put the name of the addressee just above "Dear Sir" or "Madam."

The addressee's name.

Should it be advisable to enclose in any letter an envelope for a reply, ready addressed, it is not good form to put "Esq." after one's own name in addressing it.

Enclosing reply envelopes.

Married women and widows are not addressed by their own Christian names, but by those of their husbands. For instance, no one versed in social forms would write "Mrs. Mary Smith," but "Mrs. John Smith." Widows of titled men have their Christian name put before their surname, thus, "Laura Lady Ledding," Maria Marchioness of Adesbury," Georgina Viscountess Medway," "Mary Duchess of Blankton." The unmarried daughters of dukes, marquises, and earls have their Christian name invariably inserted between their courtesy title and surname, as: "Lady Mary Baker." When married they retain this form, only substituting the husband's surname for their own, as "Lady Mary Garth." But if their

Addressing married women.

husband should be a peer, they merge
their courtesy title in his.

The third person in correspondence
is falling considerably into disuse, and
"presenting compliments" is almost
obsolete. Invitations of a formal kind,
and their replies, are couched in the
third person, but for pur-
Use of the poses of correspondence
third person. with strangers it is almost
always better to use the first person.
The exception is in replying to a letter
written in the third person, when it is
in better taste to reply in the same
way. The third person is also used in
writing to tradespeople : "Mr. Edlicott
will feel obliged if Mr. Jones will
kindly call on Thursday morning with
reference to some repairs." In this
case the reply would be written in the
first person.

Letters of introduction, says La
Fontaine, "are drafts that must be
cashed at sight." They are sometimes
difficult to write, especially if they have
been asked for, not volun-
Letters of teered. They are always
introduction. left unsealed, but should
there be circumstances about the
person introduced which the other
party should know, it is well to com-
municate them in a private letter,
which should be despatched so as to
arrive before the letter of introduction
is presented. Any one receiving a
letter of introduction would immediately take steps to show some

attention to the individual introduced.
The usual thing is to ask him to dinner,
if he is a social equal ; to offer his
services, if he should be a superior ;
and to ascertain in what way one can
be useful to him, if he is an inferior.
A personal call must precede all invitations. This is a fixed and
A call must precede invitations. rigid rule, the exception
being in the case of persons
presenting their own letters
of introduction, as is usually done.
But should the person to whom they
are addressed be out, the formal call
must follow.

All ladies, from the Queen down-
wards, are addressed in beginning a
letter as " Madam " ; all
Styles of address at the beginning of a letter. gentlemen, from the highest
to the lowest, as "Sir."
Tradesmen, however, begin
"Your Royal Highness," "Your
Grace," or "Your Ladyship," in
writing to their titled employers.
They also address their letters quite
differently, as will be seen from the
following instructions :—

ADDRESSES OF LETTERS.

Her Majesty the Queen.

To His Royal Highness the Prince
of Wales.

To Her Royal Highness the Princess
of Wales.

This same form is used in addressing
communications to all other members
of the Royal Family, adding the title

where the word "Prince" or "Princess" would be incorrect, as :—

To His Royal Highness the Duke of York.

To Her Royal Highness the Duchess of York.

Below the rank of royalty there is the distinction between letters addressed by persons on an equality with those to whom they write, and by inferiors. I shall call them formal and informal, and range them in separate lines.

Address for the envelope—formal and informal.

Informal.	Formal.
The Duke of ——	To His Grace the Duke of ——
The Duchess of ——	To Her Grace the Duchess of ——
The Marquis of ——	To the Most Honourable the Marquis of ——
The Marchioness of —	To the Most Honourable the Marchioness of ——
The Earl of ——	To the Right Honourable the Earl of ——
The Countess of ——	To the Right Honourable the Countess of ——
The Viscount ——	The Right Honourable the Viscount ——
The Viscountess ——	The Right Honourable the Viscountess——
Lord ——	The Right Honourable Lord — or Baron —
Lady ——	The Right Honourable Lady —— or Baroness ——

Members of the Privy Council are

also addressed as "Right Honourable," in the same way as Peers. In this case the names of commoners are not followed by the abbreviation "Esq.,"

Addressing Privy Councillors.

as :—

The Right Honourable James Balfour, M.P.

Ambassadors and their wives are addressed as " His Excellency," " Her Excellency," the personal and official titles following the word, as :—

Ambassadors.

To His Excellency the Earl of ——, Ambassador Extraordinary and Plenipotentiary to France.

To Her Excellency the Countess of ——.

Other official personages are addressed in the following way :—

To His Excellency Lord Blank, Lord Lieutenant of Ireland.

To His Grace the Archbishop of——.

The Right Reverend the Bishop of ——

The Very Reverend the Dean of ——.

Academical distinctions are indicated by the initials placed after the name—LL.D. for Doctor of Laws and Learning, D.D. for Doctor of Divinity and so on.

Degrees.

So much for the envelopes. The proper way to begin letters is as follows. As I have mentioned, the Queen is addressed as " Madam " in the inside of a letter. A gentleman writing

Beginning the letter.

to the Queen would sign himself, "I
have the honour to submit myself,
with profound respect, Your Majesty's
most devoted subject and
servant." Above the word
"Madam" should be written "Her
Majesty the Queen." Lord Beacons-
field struck out a line of his own and
in writing to the Queen began, "Mr.
Disraeli," continuing in the third person
and addressing Her Majesty in the
second. The Prince of Wales is
addressed as "Sir," above this word
being written "To His Royal
Highness the Prince of
Wales." Persons on inti-
mate terms sometimes begin
"Sir" or "Dear Prince," others "My
dear Prince." The Princess of Wales
is occasionally addressed by friends
as "My dear Princess." The two
orthodox endings to such letters are
respectively "Your Royal Highness's
dutiful and obedient servant," or (a
humbler style) "Your Royal Highness's
dutiful and most obedient servant."
To all other Royal Princes and
Princesses the ending would be "Most
Humble and Obedient Servant." Dukes
other than royal are addressed inside
letters by intimates as "Dear Duke,"
by others "My Lord Duke,
may it please your Grace."
In writing to a Duchess her
title is placed above the "Madam." In
formal letters Marquises would be
addressed as "My Lord Marquis."

To the Queen.

To the Prince and Princess of Wales.

To a Duke and Duchess.

A very common form of mistake is that of omitting the christian name from the courtesy titles of the sons and daughters of dukes, marquises, and earls. The sons have the title "Lord" prefixed to the christian and surname : for instance, "Lord Alfred Osborne," "Lord Henry Somerset." It is extremely incorrect to call either of these "Lord Osborne" or "Lord Somerset." The daughters of dukes, marquises and earls have the title "Lady" before their christian and surname; "Lady Emily Heneage," for instance, must not be addressed as "Lady Heneage." Should she marry a commoner only the surname is altered, the "Lady Emily" remains. This may all appear a little involved to those unaccustomed to titles, but neglect of these forms indicates very clearly a lack of *savoir faire*. It is a source of great annoyance to the owners of courtesy titles to have the christian name omitted. Anybody, even a knight's wife, may be a "Lady Smith" or "Jones"; the insertion of the christian name before the "Smith" or "Jones" means that the possessor is the daughter of a duke, marquis, or earl.

On omitting christian names from courtesy titles.

In beginning a letter to any of the above a stranger would say "Dear Lady Mary Smith," but the usual form would be "Dear Lady Mary." Inferiors would begin by writing the lady's title over the word "Madam," or

Beginning a letter to the above.

merely beginning "Madam" and writing the title at the end of the letter.

In writing to an ambassador or his wife the title is placed above the word "Sir" or "Madam." Inferiors would write "May it please your Excellency," and would conclude with "I have the honour to be Your Excellency's most humble, obedient servant."

To an ambassador, with conclusion.

In writing to an archbishop a correspondent would begin "Your Grace," ending, "I remain Your Grace's most obedient servant."

An archbishop.

To a bishop the form would be, "My Lord," or "Right Reverend Sir," or "May it please Your Lordship," the last being, of course, the humblest form of address. The conclusion would be, I remain, "My Lord" (or "Right Reverend Sir") "Your most obedient servant."

A bishop.

The beginning of a letter to a dean would be, "Reverend Sir" or "Mr. Dean," the title of all these dignitaries being, in formal letters, indited above the beginning. Those having slight acquaintance would begin, "Dear Mr. Dean." Strangers would end the letter, "I have the honour to be Your most obedient servant."

A dean.

Doctors of divinity are addressed as "Reverend Sir," as well as archdeacons and all other clergy.

Doctors of Divinity.

CORRESPONDENCE.

Intimates would begin letters to the above with : " Dear Archbishop," " Dear Bishop," " Dear Dean," or Dear Doctor."

With the sole exception of lieutenants in the army, all officers have their military rank prefixed to their name. Ensigns and lieutenants are addressed as " Esq." In the navy admirals of the flag—white, blue or red—are addressed as " The Honourable," this being prefixed to the name. Otherwise a letter would begin " Sir," and end " I remain, Sir, Your obedient servant." Commodores, captains, and lieutenants in the navy are all addressed in the same way.

Officers in the army.

And navy.

PERSONAL SPEECH WITH ROYALTY AND RANK.

It is sometimes difficult to know how to address personally people of high rank. The Queen is addressed as "Ma'am" by those immediately surrounding her person and by princesses, duchesses, and others who are on terms that may be described as those of acquaintanceship with her Majesty. All others would speak to her as "Your Majesty."

Addressing the Queen in person.

The Princess of Wales and all other princesses are in the same way addressed as "Ma'am," or "Your Royal Highness," according to the position of the person speaking to them.

The Princess of Wales.

The Prince of Wales, with all other royal dukes and princes, is addressed as "Sir," or "Your Royal Highness"; the Duke of Teck as "Your Serene Highness," as well as many foreign princes. Equals would address all these as "Prince."

The Prince of Wales and royal dukes.

The following list will show the correct modes of addressing the nobility informally and formally, in conversation, the first being the custom among acquaintances, the latter by all others :—

Formal and informal modes of addressing nobility in person.

158

PERSONAL SPEECH.

Rank.		Informal.	Formal.
Duke		Duke.	Your Grace
Duchess.	...	Duchess.	Your Grace
Marquis...	...	Lord A.	My Lord,
			or
			Your Lordship.
Marchioness...		Lady A.	My Lady,
			or
			Your Ladyship.
Earl		Lord B.	My Lord,
			or
			Your Lordship.
Countess	...	Lady B.	My Lady,
			or
			Your Ladyship.
Viscount	...	Lord C.	My Lord,
			or
			Your Lordship.
Viscountess ...		Lady C.	My Lady,
			or
			Your Ladyship.
Baron		Lord D.	My Lord,
			or
			Your Lordship.
Baroness	...	Lady D.	My Lady,
			or
			Your Ladyship

It is one of the rules of etiquette that, in speaking with royal persons, the inferior leaves it to them to originate subjects of conversation, and never introduces any topic of his own.

Letters of condolence are among the most difficult forms of composition.

Letters of condolence. They are almost equally trying to read and to write. The best rule to be given for these is to make them as brief as possible. If "brevity is the soul of wit," it is also, in such cases, the very heart of sympathy. A very usual fault committed is to begin by dilating upon the shock or grief felt by the writer. The absurdity of this becomes apparent when one compares mentally the shock or grief as felt by the recipient. Two lines conveying the expression of sympathy are better than pages of even the most eloquent composition. Mourners require all their fortitude at times of loss, and anything likely to impair their self-command is the reverse of a kindness.

On hearing or reading of the death of an acquaintance or friend, an expression of sympathy should at once be sent off. It used to be the custom to wait for the memoriam **Memoriam cards.** cards sent out by the family, but this, if it was ever the custom in the best society, has now long ceased to be so. Memoriam cards are only used in humble circles. At the same time, one needs to be very careful as to the accuracy of one's information before sending off a letter of condolence. Similarity of name is apt to lead to awkward mistakes. In this connection it may be as well to remark that about a week after the funeral it is customary to **The inquiry call.** call and leave cards of inquiry. When these are responded to by cards of thanks for inquiries, it is a sign that the family is willing to receive callers.

UNWIN BROTHERS, PRINTERS, WOKING AND LONDON.

Rowland's Odonto

The best and safest Dentifrice : whitens the teeth, prevents decay : no grit nor ruinous acids. 2/9.

Rowland's Macassar Oil

Absolutely the only reliable and genuine Preserver, Restorer, and Strengthener of the Hair : also in a Golden Colour. Bottles, 3/6, 7/-, and 10/6.

Rowland's Kalydor

Beautifies the Complexion : produces Soft, Fair Skin : removes all Disfigurements : warranted Harmless. 2/3 and 4/6, of all Perfumery Dealers.

Send Postal Order to

A. ROWLAND & SONS, 20, HATTON GARDEN, LONDON.

NEW ILLUSTRATED BOOK.

"WHAT GALVANISM HAS DONE AND IS DOING."

Many interesting and instructive lectures on Electricity are given by the most eminent scientific men of the present day. All are agreed as to its curative properties and power to relieve pain, and call attention to the many fraudulent appliances offered to the public, but they do not state where one may obtain a genuine appliance constructed on the necessary principles of the continuous current.

Our New Book explains clearly and very simply how to test an electrical appliance, either Battery or Belt, to prove its efficacy. It will instruct you—

HOW GALVANISM CURES LUMBAGO AND PAIN IN BACK.

HOW GALVANISM CURES LOCAL WEAKNESS FROM ALL CAUSES.

HOW GALVANISM CURES ANÆMIA AND BAD CIRCULATION.

HOW GALVANISM CURES ASTHMA, BRONCHITIS, GOUT, AND RHEUMATISM.

HOW GALVANISM CURES CHILDREN IN DELICATE HEALTH.

To be had post free on mentioning this Book, from—

J. L. PULVERMACHER & CO., Lᵀᴰ

194, REGENT STREET, W.

Miss Frances E. Willard says :—" This beautiful and helpful book will do enormous good in this age when faith is weak."

The Sketch says :—" Mr. Coulson Kernahan is a man of very large imaginative gifts. He is a dreamer of dreams, yet human love begets them. There are few delivering an apocalypse to-day who have a tithe of his literary skill. He affects nothing, seeking rather to appeal to the heart of his reader, and in his simplicity finds his strength. How great that strength is a perusal of 'The Child, the Wise Man, and the Devil' very clearly shows. . . . As dramatic and as finely realised as anything in the fiction of to-day. '. . . A masterpiece of prose and imagination."

The Rev. F. B. Meyer says :—" It is powerfully conceived, and thrills with passion ; but its chief value is its exposure of the hopelessness and impossibility of the goal to which modern infidelity would conduct us. It will arrest and convince thousands."

The Rev. Canon H. D. Rawnsley says :—" This noble parable."

The Illustrated London News says :—"All, of whatever school, must recognise the boundless charity, the literary power, and the intense sincerity of one of the most interesting books of the year."

The Rev. Hugh Price Hughes says :—" I recognised in it at once Mr. Kernahan's striking genius. I have no doubt that he will reach many who cannot be approached by any of the ordinary agencies or modes. From every point of view I regard it as a very valuable and remarkable book."

The Rev. Morlais Jones :—" The Rev. Morlais Jones preached an interesting sermon on Sunday last," says the *British Weekly.* " Mr. Morlais Jones referred in terms of enthusiastic praise to Mr. Coulson Kernahan's new book, 'The Child, the Wise Man, and the Devil.' The author, he said, was a man of unmistakable genius."

The Echo says :—" Let us acknowledge with gratitude the fine moral enthusiasm, the lofty spiritual fervour, and the chivalrous charity of this most poetic of prosemen. The writer is manly, vigorous, and sincere. . . . There will be few readers of this work, however thoroughly they may dissent from the author's contentions, who will not allow with enthusiasm the moral earnestness, the poetic imagination, and the literary charm of Mr. Kernahan's stern muse."

LONDON : JAMES BOWDEN, HENRIETTA STREET, W.C.

Old London Cries

A quality reprint of an 1885 edition with over 140 pages of informative and interesting reading, together with over 50 woodcuts depicting various street traders of London from the seventeenth century.

Price
£7.95

"Beautifully illustrated"—*London's City Recorder*

Manners for Women

"A useful reminder that tittering is an unpleasant habit and that courtsying should be avoided unless you know what you are doing.

FIRST PUBLISHED 1897; OWING TO DEMAND IS BEING REPUBLISHED." —THE TIMES, *July 1993*

HAND SHADOWS
TO BE THROWN UPON THE WALL:
CONSISTING OF NOVEL AND AMUSING FIGURES FORMED BY THE HAND.

Price
£3.99

Size: 9½" x 7"
ISBN 0 946014 248
Paperback 48pp

Most of us will remember something about hand shadows from our childhood. Today this delightful, amusing and educational pastime is sadly neglected, but in this fascinating Victorian book, first published in 1860, the subject is explored in full with delightful good size illustrations. For children and adults of all ages, here is the perfect antidote to today's rush and bustle.

"What Shall I Say?"

A guide to letter writing for ladies first published in 1898, this book covers all aspects of letter writing from complaining of being attacked by a vicious dog, to a lover complaining of coldness.

Price
£3.99

ISBN 0946014 25 6

published in the spring of 1994

Available from bookshops or post free from
PRYOR PUBLICATIONS
75 Dargate Road, Yorkletts, Whitstable, Kent CT5 3AE, England.
Tel. & Fax: (0227) 274655
A full list of our publications sent free on request.